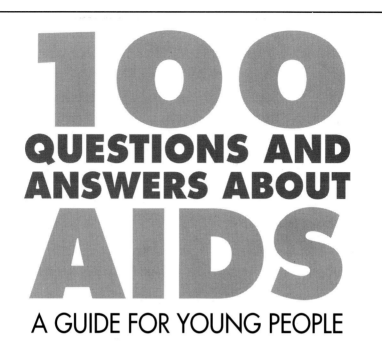

100 QUESTIONS AND ANSWERS ABOUT AIDS

A GUIDE FOR YOUNG PEOPLE

MICHAEL THOMAS FORD

AN OPEN DOOR BOOK

new
Discovery
B·O·O·K·S

New York

Maxwell Macmillan Canada
Toronto

Maxwell Macmillan International
New York   Oxford   Singapore   Sydney

Front cover design: Carol Matsuyama
Interior design, layout and production: Deborah Fillion
Condom use and needle cleaning diagrams: Kathie Kelleher

New Discovery Books
Macmillan Publishing Company
866 Third Avenue
New York, NY 10022

Maxwell Macmillan Canada, Inc.
1200 Eglinton Avenue East
Suite 200
Don Mills, Ontario M3C 3N1

Macmillan Publishing Company is part of the Maxwell Communication Group of Companies.

Printed in the United States of America

10 9 8 7 6 5 4 3 2

The author wishes to thank the following for permission to reprint lyrics from "Walk and Talk Like Angels":

"Walk and Talk Like Angels"
Words and Music by Toni Childs and David Ricketts
Copyright © 1988 by MCA Music Publishing, a division of MCA Inc., Moon Skin Music, Almo Music Corporation, and 48/11 Music. Rights of Moon Skin Music administered by MCA Music Publishing, a division of MCA Music, Inc. New York, N.Y. 10019. Used by permission. All rights reserved.

"Walk and Talk Like Angels"
Words and Music by David Ricketts and Toni Childs
Copyright © 1988 Almo Music Corp. & 48/11 Music and Unicity Music, Inc. and Moon Skin Music (ASCAP). All rights reserved. International copyright secured.

Library of Congress Cataloging-in-Publication Data
Ford, Michael Thomas
        100 questions and answers about AIDS : a guide for young people / Michael Thomas Ford — 1st ed.
            p.   cm. — (An open door book)
        Includes index.
        Summary: Answers 100 common questions about AIDS, what causes it, how it is spread, and how to protect yourself from getting it. Includes interviews with four young people living with HIV infection.
        ISBN 0-02-735424-5
        1. AIDS (Disease) — Miscellanea — Juvenile literature. [1. AIDS (Disease) — Miscellanea. 2. Questions and answers.] I. Title. II. Title: One hundred questions and answers about AIDS. II. Series: Open door book.
RC607.A2F65 1992
616.97'92—dc20   92-15072

for those who
told their stories

you walk like the angels talk
where are you from
you want to walk and talk like the
    angels talk
tell me then some

with a room by the sea
and a voice in the sand
telling me your truth
and telling me your view
in how you see the world
spinning, spinning round
and what is love and what is death
the fears you have to put to rest
and so you walk
like the angels talk

— *from "walk and talk like angels"*
by Toni Childs and David Ricketts

CONTENTS

In 1981, when the first cases of what we now call AIDS were reported in the news, I was in high school, not much older than many of you reading this book. In fact, the first time I heard about AIDS was when it was assigned as the topic for a term paper in one of my English classes.

At that time, AIDS was still called "gay cancer" because it seemed to be affecting only homosexual men in San Francisco and Los Angeles. In the small farming community where I lived, no one thought AIDS was a real concern, and certainly it would never touch anyone we knew. When I went to the library to gather information for my term paper, I thought how lucky I was that I would never know anyone with AIDS.

In the years that followed, AIDS continued to spread. It was there day after day, every time I turned on the nightly news or opened a magazine. The numbers grew higher and higher, and soon it was apparent that AIDS was not going to go away. But it still seemed like I was watching reports of a foreign war, something that was happening somewhere far away to other people. The men and women who appeared on television to talk about AIDS were not people I knew, and I really didn't want to get too close to a disease that could do the horrible things AIDS was doing to the people I saw on the talk shows and the news.

Then I moved to New York and started doing volunteer work in the lesbian and gay community. In a very short time, I met many people for whom AIDS was not just a nightly news report but an everyday reality. Suddenly AIDS was not just something that happened to other people, it was something that happened to people I cared very much about. It was as if I had been dropped right into the middle of the battle I had once viewed safely from a distance.

That was several years ago, and since then I have learned a great deal about AIDS—more, in fact, than I ever wanted to know. The medical facts are easy—what AIDS is, how it is transmitted, how to prevent it. But learning the facts doesn't prepare you for the reality of AIDS—watching a friend get sicker and sicker every week; asking about someone you haven't seen in a few months and being told that he has died; finding a home for someone's dog because she is too sick to care for him anymore.

Because I live in New York, I am closer to the AIDS epidemic than many people. I see firsthand the demonstrations by AIDS activist groups like ACT UP and WHAM!. I pass the posters demanding increased AIDS funding from the government that are plastered all over my Greenwich Village neighborhood. I walk by Katie, the homeless woman who sits near the West Fourth Street subway entrance with the sign that says, "Homeless with AIDS. Please Help." If I have any change, I drop it into the coffee cup next to her and ask how she is. The answer is always the same: "Still livin'."

Many of you reading this book don't see the effects of AIDS every day. Your vision of AIDS is of a group of angry women and men screaming on the steps of a building in Washington, D.C., or marching in the streets of New York or San Francisco chanting and waving signs. You might not know anyone living with HIV, the virus that causes AIDS, and you don't understand why those people protesting and marching seem so angry.

Those men and women are fighting. They are fighting a battle for their lives, for the lives of friends, brothers, lovers, mothers, fathers, and sisters, for the lives of everyone touched by AIDS. They are screaming because they want to make people understand that AIDS will not go away, and that it is killing people of every color, age, and sex. They are angry because they know what living with AIDS really means; that it doesn't go away when you turn off the television or close the newspaper.

The young people whose stories you will read in this book didn't think AIDS could happen to them either. Like myself, and like many of you, they heard about AIDS on the news and read about it in newspapers and magazines. And like myself, they thought how lucky they were not to have AIDS.

Now they are fighting the disease they never thought they could get. Some have been fighting for many years, others for only a short time. They have each responded differently to having HIV, and each one has had to deal with her or his own issues and emotions. Listen to what they have to say.

* * *

Writing this book has been one of the most rewarding things I have ever done. The people I have met and who have helped me put this project together have become friends, and it is their phone calls, letters, and words of encouragement that have brought it all together.

Thank you to the following people for their patience in listening to my questions and their help in directing me to people who knew the answers: Dr. Larry Millhofer, Nancy Evans, Julie Graham and the great kids at Bay Area Young Positives, Patty Glynn, Christina Lewis, Lee Kearney, the staff at the National AIDS Hotline, Jenny Hincks, Victoria Brownworth, Shed Boren and Tim Koontz of Body Positive, Patty Manning, John McIlveen, Polly Hill O'Keefe, Dr. Mervyn F. Silverman, and everyone out there making sure that young people get the message.

Special thanks to Peter McKie, Emma Dryden, Susan Grossman, Frank Sloan, Kathy Solomon Probosz, Krista Blake, Mary Cresse, Kathryn Hinds, Rebecca Pieken, and Rosemary Grillo, who reminded me from time to time that it was all worth it.

—*Michael Thomas Ford*
New York
March 1992

In early 1981, five previously healthy young gay men were seen at a clinic in Los Angeles. Each had symptoms that appeared to be the result of damaged immune systems. This was unusual because none of the men had anything in their medical histories to explain their conditions. Shortly after these cases were reported, in June of that year, other physicians around the country began to realize that they, too, were seeing similar cases in young men.

Because this unusual condition was seen almost exclusively in gay men, it was first called Gay Related Immune Deficiency, or GRID. Attempts were made to understand why gay men seemed to be the only ones affected by this mysterious condition and what it was that was putting them at risk for acquiring the disease. Initially, no one knew what was causing the problem, nor how it was getting into the bodies of these young men.

It soon became clear that whatever was causing this condition was transmitted through sexual activity and, as cases began showing up among injection-drug users, through the use of contaminated needles. Also noted were cases among individuals who had received blood transfusions or blood products, particularly hemophiliacs. Since people other than gay men were now being diagnosed, the official name of the condition became Acquired Immun-odeficiency Syndrome, or AIDS. With record speed, the organism causing AIDS was identified as a virus and a test was developed to determine whether or not a person had been infected.

More than a decade later, with over 200,000 reported cases of AIDS in the United States alone, we know the following about the disease:

1. No one is immune to the AIDS virus. It is an equal-opportunity infector that doesn't care whether you are old or young, gay or straight, male or female, black or white, brown or yellow.

2. The virus is not casually spread like a cold or the flu.

3. An infected woman can infect her unborn child.

4. The virus can be spread by having unprotected sex or sharing needles or syringes with an infected person. If people do not engage in unprotected sex or share nee-dles and syringes, they can avoid AIDS.

5. A person can be infected by receiving a contaminated blood transfusion or blood products, or an infected organ. By testing and discarding contaminated blood, blood products, and organs, the risk of being infected in these ways can be almost eliminated.

While these facts seem quite simple, many people still do not understand them, and today—over ten years after the first cases were diagnosed—they deny that they could get infected and continue to place themselves and others at risk through unprotected sex and the sharing of needles and syringes.

Many of us are guilty of practicing denial when it comes to risky behavior. We assume that we are somehow immune to auto accidents, sexually transmitted diseases, or the cancer-causing contents of cigarettes. These things only happen to "other people." The fact is that every year in the United States the number of "other people" equals: over 40,000 men, women, and children who die in auto accidents; millions who get sexually transmitted diseases; and over 400,000 who die from the effects of smoking.

And every ten minutes, another person is diagnosed with AIDS. Soon everyone will know at least one person infected with the AIDS virus. Already there are over 1 million people worldwide with AIDS and over 8 million who are infected with HIV, the virus that causes AIDS. At the present rate, by the year 2000, 40 million people will be infected, among them 10 million young people. Another 10 million kids who are not infected will soon become orphans because AIDS will have killed their parents.

AIDS is a powerful enemy, but there is something we can do to fight it. Even without any medicines or vaccines, we can stop the spread of this disease. By knowing the facts about AIDS and practicing safe behavior, you can remain free of AIDS. This book clearly answers 100 often-asked questions about HIV and AIDS. It also includes interviews with people your age who have been infected. Please read it carefully. If you have further questions, refer to the Resource Guide for telephone numbers of community organizations that can help you.

You have the power within you to remain free of AIDS. You also have the ability to show compassion toward those who have unfortunately already become infected with the AIDS virus. Think of how you would like to be treated if you had AIDS, and it will be easy to be sensitive to the needs of those afflicted with this terrible disease.

AIDS is everyone's problem, and everyone can be part of the solution.

—Mervyn F. Silverman, MD, MPH
President, American Foundation for
AIDS Research
San Francisco, California
March 1992

The following is a list of all the questions contained in this book. Because the answers to some questions depend on information found in other questions, it is recommended that you read all of the questions rather than just the ones you might be interested in. Reading the answers to only the questions you care about will not give you all of the information that you need to know about HIV and AIDS.

SECTION ONE: HIV & AIDS
1. What is AIDS?
2. What causes AIDS?
3. How does HIV cause AIDS?
4. What causes death in a person with AIDS?
5. What are some of the opportunistic infections that most often affect people with AIDS?
6. Why doesn't the immune system destroy HIV?
7. How is HIV different from a cold or flu virus?
8. If AIDS is not transmitted through casual contact, how is it transmitted?
9. Is HIV found only in blood?
10. Is HIV found in any other bodily substances?
11. Does everyone exposed to HIV contract the virus?
12. How many people are infected with HIV?
13. How many young people have HIV?

14. How long after contracting HIV do the first signs of infection develop?
15. What are the early symptoms of HIV infection?
16. Are the symptoms of HIV infection the same for women and men?
17. What is the difference between being HIV-positive and having full-blown AIDS?
18. Why is the CDC definition of full-blown AIDS so important?
19. How long after being infected with HIV does full-blown AIDS develop?
20. Does everyone infected with HIV develop full-blown AIDS?
21. How many people have AIDS?
22. How many young people have AIDS?
23. How do we know how many people in the United States have AIDS?
24. Do all people with AIDS die?
25. How did AIDS start?
26. Is AIDS a problem in other countries?
27. Is there a vaccine for AIDS?

SECTION TWO: FACT & FICTION

28. Can I get AIDS from toilet seats or silverware or from shaking hands or kissing a person with AIDS?
29. Don't only people in certain "risk groups" get AIDS?
30. My friend is gay, and I've heard that a lot of homosexuals get AIDS. Should I worry that he has AIDS?
31. Isn't AIDS a problem only in big cities, like New York and San Francisco?
32. Can a person be born with AIDS?

33. Can an infected woman pass the virus to her baby through breast-feeding even if the baby is born without the virus?
34. Can the AIDS virus pass through the skin?
35. Someone at my school has AIDS. Should I be afraid to talk to her?
36. What if someone with the virus coughs or sneezes near me?
37. My friends say that you can't get AIDS the first time you have sex. Is this true?
38. Can I get AIDS from my doctor or dentist?
39. What is the risk of getting AIDS from a blood transfusion or organ transplant?
40. Can I get AIDS from donating blood?
41. Can I get AIDS from performing CPR on someone with AIDS?
42. Can mosquitoes, ticks, or other biting insects transmit the virus?
43. Can I contract the AIDS virus by having my ears pierced or getting a tattoo?
44. I can always tell if someone is infected, can't I?
45. Married people don't get AIDS, do they?
46. Can people with HIV infection still have sex?
47. Isn't it dangerous to have people with HIV on a sports team?

SECTION THREE: KEEPING SAFE

48. Why is AIDS called a sexually transmitted disease?
49. What is meant by the term *sexual contact?*
50. How is HIV spread through vaginal sex?
51. How is HIV spread through anal sex?
52. How is HIV spread through oral sex?

53. Is the person receiving oral sex also at risk?
54. Is oral sex really that risky?
55. Is all sex dangerous?
56. What are some safer sex practices?
57. What is a condom?
58. How do you use a condom?
59. Do all types of condoms offer protection against the transmission of HIV?
60. Are condoms 100% effective?
61. What do I do if a condom breaks?
62. How can I protect myself during oral sex?
63. I'm too embarrassed to buy condoms. What can I do?
64. What can I do if my religion prohibits the use of condoms?
65. My partner says that if I love him I won't make him wear condoms. What should I do?
66. How can I talk to my partner about safer sex?
67. How do I say no to risky behavior?
68. How do drugs and alcohol affect risky behavior?
69. My friends say that "real" men don't wear condoms. I don't want to look dumb, so what can I do?
70. Can spermicides kill the AIDS virus?
71. Is being on the pill or using a diaphragm enough to protect me from the AIDS virus?
72. Will douching after sex kill the AIDS virus?
73. Is pulling out before ejaculation safe?
74. Is deep, or French, kissing okay?
75. I've been with the same partner for two years. Do we have to worry?
76. How is HIV spread by using needles?
77. I use intravenous drugs. How can I keep safe?

SECTION FOUR: TESTING & BEYOND

78. How can I find out if I am infected with HIV?
79. Who should be tested for HIV?
80. What will an HIV test tell me?
81. How soon after a person is infected with HIV will the virus show up in a test?
82. Where can I get an HIV antibody test?
83. What is the difference between the different places offering HIV tests?
84. What are the different types of tests for HIV?
85. What will happen when I go for an HIV test?
86. What does a positive HIV test result mean?
87. What does a negative or inconclusive HIV test result mean?
88. Isn't it better not to know if you have HIV?
89. Can an HIV test result be wrong?
90. How often should I be tested for HIV?
91. Why do some people say that there should be mandatory HIV testing?
92. What do I do if I am HIV-positive?
93. What is done to treat people with HIV and AIDS?
94. Who can I talk to about HIV and AIDS?
95. Why do some people say that people with AIDS deserve the disease?
96. Someone I know has AIDS, and now my friends don't want me to talk to him. How can I tell them it's okay?
97. My brother is HIV-positive, and I'm afraid to tell anyone. How can I deal with my feelings?
98. My six-year-old sister wants to know about AIDS. What should I tell her?
99. What should I say when someone tells me she or he is infected with HIV?
100. What can I do about AIDS?

HIV & **AIDS**

1.
What is AIDS?

AIDS stands for a condition called **acquired immunodeficiency syndrome**. This is a very long name, but it is easy to understand if you take the different parts one at a time.

The word *acquired* tells us that AIDS is something that a person gets, or acquires, from another person. Although AIDS can be passed from an infected woman to her unborn child (there is more about this in later sections), it is not something that you inherit from your parents like your height or the color of your hair or eyes. It is also not an illness that can occur with no apparent outward cause, as cancer is, or that is a result of the body's aging process, like Alzheimer's disease.

Immunodeficiency is another long word, but it, too, is easy if you take it apart. *Immuno* refers to the body's **immune system**. The immune system is the part of the body that fights off infections. When your body is invaded by organisms that cause diseases like measles, the flu, or colds, the immune system prevents you from getting sick by attacking and destroying these organisms. A *deficiency* means that there is a lack of something, or not enough of it to work correctly. So, *immunodeficiency* means that a person's immune system is not strong enough to work correctly and is lacking the ability to fight off disease-causing organisms that, normally, it would destroy easily.

The last word, *syndrome*, means a group of conditions or symptoms that show, or indicate, that something is wrong. If you put these three words together, you get a good definition of AIDS. A person with AIDS has a group of conditions or symptoms (syndrome) that indicate that she or he has become infected with (acquired) a virus that is causing the immune system to become weakened to the point where substances that would normally be destroyed are now able to survive and cause infections and diseases (immunodeficiency).

2.
What causes AIDS?

AIDS is caused by a virus called **HIV**. HIV stands for **human immunodeficiency virus**. If we look at each part of this word, we will get a definition, as we did for AIDS.

In this case, we will start with the last word, *virus*. A virus is a very small organism that invades a person's body and causes disease. Different viruses cause different illnesses. For instance, the flu virus causes the flu and the measles virus causes measles. In this case, the virus HIV causes AIDS.

We already know that *immunodeficiency* means

that a person has a weakened immune system. If we link this to the word *virus*, we know that HIV is a virus that causes immunodeficiency, a breakdown in the body's immune system.

The first part of HIV, *human*, lets us know that this is a virus that affects only people, not animals. Putting this all together, we can determine that HIV is a virus that causes the condition of immunodeficiency in humans.

When a person has been infected by the AIDS virus, we say that she or he is **HIV-positive**, or **seropositive**. This means that the person's blood has tested positive for the presence of HIV. Since their discovery, both HIV and AIDS have been called different things at different times. Since AIDS is caused by HIV, many people simply call it **HIV disease**. Throughout this book, the virus that causes AIDS will be referred to as either *HIV* or *the AIDS virus*.

3.
How does HIV cause AIDS?

HIV causes AIDS by weakening a person's immune system. The immune system is made up of different parts, each of which has a different job in fighting infections. When a person is infected by HIV, the virus enters the bloodstream, which is part of the immune system. HIV then begins to attack parts of the immune system. In particular, HIV invades and destroys **T4–lymphocytes** (commonly called T–cells or **helper lymphocytes**) and

macrophages, two types of white blood cells that are very important in fighting off infections. A virus is much smaller than a blood cell, so HIV is able to enter T–cells and macrophages and live inside them.

HIV then uses the **genetic material** found in these cells to reproduce itself. In a process called **transcription**, a cell reads the codes found in its genetic material and makes a perfect copy of itself. What HIV does is interrupt the transcription process and trick a healthy cell into producing a copy of the AIDS virus rather than a copy of itself. In effect, it turns a healthy cell into a factory that produces copies of the AIDS virus. Eventually, HIV destroys the cell that it has invaded and moves on to another cell. When enough of these cells are destroyed, the body is unable to fight infections.

HIV may also spread to the **central nervous system**, the system of the body that includes the brain and spinal cord and is involved in muscle movement, eyesight, and other functions. When the central nervous system is infected with HIV, vision, coordination, muscle control, and memory may all be affected.

A good example of how HIV works can be seen in what is called the **T-cell count**. This is a test that tells how many T4-cells a person has per cubic millimeter of blood. A person with a healthy immune system will have a T-cell count ranging from 600–1500. As HIV infection progresses, the T-cell count falls lower and lower as the AIDS virus destroys more and more healthy cells. Because the T4-cell is an important part of the immune system, as the T-cell count drops, the body's ability to fight off infections is decreased. Because the immune system is weakened, or suppressed, this condition is called **immunosuppression**. As immunosuppression continues and the T-cell count drops below 200, organisms that normally would be destroyed by the immune system are able to infect the body. These infections are called **opportunistic infections** because they take the opportunity offered by immunosuppression to enter the body.

Generally, the lower a person's T-cell count is, the more immunosuppressed he or she becomes. T-cell counts are helpful in predicting the progression of HIV infection and in monitoring a person's response to treatment.

4.
What causes death in a person with AIDS?

As HIV destroys more and more cells in the immune system, it is easier for opportunistic infections and cancers to invade the body. People with AIDS may get many opportunistic infections during the course of their illness, either one at a time or several at once. Eventually, the immune system is so suppressed that one or more of these infections or cancers develops and cannot be treated successfully. When we say that someone has died of AIDS, we mean that she or he has died as a result of one of these opportunistic infections or cancers.

5.

What are some of the opportunistic infections that most often affect people with AIDS?

Any disease can more easily infect a person with immunosuppression than it can a person with a healthy immune system, so people with AIDS are affected by a great many different diseases. However, there are several diseases that seem to regularly affect people with AIDS and account for a majority of AIDS-related deaths.

The disease that most frequently causes death in people with AIDS is ***Pneumocystis carinii* pneumonia (PCP)**, which accounts for almost one third of all AIDS-related deaths. PCP is an infection that invades the lungs and causes pneumonia, a disease that fills the lungs with fluid and makes breathing very difficult. In a person with a healthy immune system, pneumonia can be treated fairly easily. But in a person suffering from immunosuppression, pneumonia cannot be treated effectively and often causes death.

Another disease that often kills people infected with HIV is **Kaposi's sarcoma (KS)**, a rare form of cancer that was almost never seen in the Western Hemisphere before the start of the AIDS **epidemic**. KS is a type of skin cancer. It most often appears as purplish splotches on a person's skin that start off as small spots and grow to the size of a dime or larger. It is a very difficult cancer to treat and spreads quickly once it has begun. KS affects almost exclusively men and is not often found in women with AIDS. Lately, the number of deaths from KS has begun to slow down, and it is expected that it will eventually account for a much smaller percentage of AIDS-related deaths.

While these diseases frequently cause death in people with AIDS in the United States, it is impossible to say that people with AIDS tend to die from one disease more than another. While KS is becoming less of a problem, for example, **tuberculosis**, a disease that affects various parts of the body, mainly the lungs, and causes the infected person to lose enormous amounts of weight, is accounting for an increasing number of deaths in people with HIV infection. And in Africa, the majority of AIDS deaths are a result of malnutrition and severe weight loss from chronic diarrhea. As the AIDS crisis continues, we will probably see many shifts in the opportunistic infections that affect people with HIV disease.

6.
Why doesn't the immune system destroy HIV?

Normally, when a virus invades the body, the immune system recognizes the virus and produces **antibodies**, special proteins that are designed to attack and destroy foreign substances. For instance, when your body is attacked by a flu virus, your immune system recognizes the presence of the flu virus and generates antibodies that are equipped to destroy flu viruses. The immune system also mobilizes special cells called **killer lymphocytes,** which can attack both the invading virus and cells invaded by the virus. The T-cells we discussed earlier help antibody-forming cells to recognize foreign invaders. They also release certain substances that attract other immune cells to the site of infection.

When HIV destroys the T-cells, it is actually destroying the generals that run the battle between the immune system and the invading substances. Without their leaders, the other cells of the immune system become confused. They don't know which cells to attack, and the defenses fall.

To make things worse, the AIDS virus may enter a cell and become dormant, waiting inside the cell to be used at a later time. It can stay there as long as six months without the body recognizing its presence. HIV is also able to mutate, or change its form, very easily. This makes it very difficult for the immune system to design an effective plan of attack. The immune system forms defenses based on the invading substance's structure. When that structure changes, whatever defenses have been designed become useless. When HIV mutates, the lymphocytes that have been programmed to attack and kill it no longer recognize it, and the AIDS virus can move freely throughout the body until new defenses are created.

7.
How is HIV different from a cold or flu virus?

HIV is similar to the viruses that cause colds and the flu only in that it can be passed from one person to another. But while it is very easy to contract a cold or flu virus, it is difficult to contract HIV. A virus like a cold or flu virus is **contagious**, meaning that it can be transmitted from one person to another through **casual contact**, or everyday exposure. If someone with a cold sneezes, the cold virus is released into the air in droplets of moisture. If someone else breathes the droplets in, he or she can catch the cold. Similarly, if someone with the flu coughs or sneezes, the flu virus can remain on the skin or on the surfaces of near-by objects. If someone else uses these objects or shakes hands with the infected person, she or he can be exposed to the flu virus. Soon the virus can have spread to many people. This is why it is not unusual for many people in a school or office to get a cold or the flu at the same time.

HIV is very different. Although it can be passed from one person to another, it cannot be spread through casual contact. Whereas the cold or flu virus is very strong and can live outside the body for long periods in air, water, food, or on surfaces of objects, HIV is extremely fragile. There is no way the virus could live on a water fountain or a toilet seat. You cannot breathe HIV in if someone sneezes or get it from touching an infected person's skin. Instead, we say that AIDS is **transmissible**. This means that it *can* be passed from one person to another, but *not* through casual contact.

8.

If AIDS is not transmitted through casual contact, how is it transmitted?

HIV is transmitted *only* when the virus comes into direct contact with someone's bloodstream. This can happen primarily in four ways: through sexual intercourse, by using infected needles and syringes to inject **intravenous drugs** or **steroids**, from an infected mother to her unborn baby, or by receiving infected blood or blood products. There is more detailed information on each of these modes of transmission in later sections of this book.

9.

Is HIV found only in blood?

When a person is infected with HIV, the virus will be present in one or more of his or her **bodily fluids**. The bodily fluids most likely to contain HIV are blood, semen, vaginal secretions, and breast milk. **Semen** is the fluid that is emitted from a man's **penis** when he ejaculates during sexual activity. It is commonly referred to as **cum**. There is also a clear fluid that is produced by a man's penis prior to ejaculation called **pre-cum**. HIV may be present in pre-cum. **Vaginal secretions** are the liquids that are manufactured within a woman's **vagina**. **Breast milk** is the milk produced by a woman's body during pregnancy and secreted by the breasts to feed a baby after it is born.

10.
Is HIV found in any other bodily substances?

HIV has been found in **saliva**, tears, and sweat of some infected people, but in such small amounts that coming into contact with these fluids is not dangerous. HIV has also been found in the **urine** of some people infected with HIV, though it is very unlikely that contact with an infected person's urine will cause transmission. The **feces**, or bowel movements, of infected people may contain blood, and it is theoretically possible that HIV could be transmitted by this means, since the blood of an infected person always contains the AIDS virus; but the risk is only slightly more than that in coming into contact with tears or saliva.

Although it is highly unlikely that a person will become infected by touching the bodily fluids of someone with the AIDS virus, HIV can enter the bloodstream through cuts or sores on the hands or other parts of the body, so people who care for AIDS patients may wear rubber gloves when handling clothes, sheets, or bandages that have come into contact with bodily substances. This prevents any infected material from coming into contact with broken skin.

11.
Does everyone exposed to HIV contract the virus?

It is impossible to say what percentage of people exposed to HIV will contract the virus. Just as not everyone exposed to the viruses that cause typhoid fever, colds, or other diseases automatically catches these diseases, the AIDS virus doesn't automatically infect everyone who comes into contact with it. Some people have been exposed to the AIDS virus many times without contracting it; others have been exposed only once and become infected. This does not, however, mean that certain people are immune to HIV or can't be infected by the virus. Everyone can become infected with HIV.

12.
How many people are infected with HIV?

As of December 31, 1991, the Centers for Disease Control (CDC) estimates that there are between 1 and 1.5 million people in the United States infected with HIV. The CDC is an organization based in Atlanta, Georgia, that monitors the spread of many different diseases, including AIDS. The World Health Organization, which collects data on diseases throughout the world, estimates that there are between 11 and 12 million people worldwide carrying the AIDS virus. It is impossible to get an exact number of people who have HIV because many people don't know they are infected. Also, many people do not go for testing either because they are afraid or because they mistakenly believe that they are not at risk for becoming infected with HIV.

13.
How many young people have HIV?

It is estimated that there are between 1 and 2 million people under the age of 20 infected worldwide. It is impossible, however, to really estimate the number of young people who are infected. There is still the belief among many young people that they can't get HIV. Therefore, a lot of them do not get tested, and many who are walking around with the virus don't have any idea that they are infected and won't find out until they are older and the disease has had time to develop. Many of the people who are just now being diagnosed with AIDS are between 20 and 25, which indicates that they were most likely infected when they were teenagers. The CDC estimates that as many as 25% of these people were infected between the ages of 13 and 19.

There are also a large number of homeless, or street, teenagers in the United States who are thought to be infected with HIV. Because these young people usually do not have access to medical facilities, they are often not tested for HIV. If these young people were included in the estimates, the numbers would probably be much higher. Until young people start to get tested at an earlier age and more services are provided for homeless people, we will never know for sure how many young people have the AIDS virus.

14.
How long after contracting HIV do the first signs of infection develop?

Some people develop an acute flulike syndrome, similar to mononucleosis, within two to three weeks of becoming infected with HIV. This is then followed by a long period during which the person is **asymptomatic**, or has no symptoms at all. This period can last for many years. This is dangerous because during this time an infected person may unknowingly pass the virus on to other people. During this asymptomatic period, the virus will continue to multiply. Finally, maybe as long as eight to ten years after the initial infection, the person will once again develop symptoms of HIV infection.

15.
What are the early symptoms of HIV infection?

The symptoms of HIV infection are similar to many of the symptoms that accompany common illnesses. The difference between the symptoms of HIV infection and the symptoms of common illnesses is that the symptoms of HIV infection will last much longer than those for common illnesses and will be much more severe. For instance, having diarrhea is not uncommon. But people infected with HIV may have diarrhea very frequently with no apparent cause. Swollen glands are a common symptom of having the flu. But having swollen glands in several parts of your body for no reason may be a symptom of HIV infection. A chart of common symptoms of HIV infection is shown below.

Possible symptoms of HIV infection include:

- Very high fevers (over 103°) that last for more than three to five days
- A cough that brings up fluid from the lungs and lasts several weeks
- Purplish blotches on the skin that are not the result of contact with irritating chemicals
- Sores and infections that will not go away even after medical treatment
- Tiredness or weakness that lasts for many weeks without explanation
- **Lymph nodes** in at least two sites on the body that are swollen to marble-size or larger
- Rapid weight loss (10 pounds or more) that is not the result of dieting
- Painful or thick whitish coating in the mouth, vagina, or rectum with no apparent cause
- Repeated colds, flus, or flulike symptoms that last for days at a time and recur frequently
- Frequent diarrhea that has no apparent cause

As the T-cell count drops from 500 to 200, the HIV-infected person may develop minor symptoms like fatigue, headaches, diarrhea, fevers, or night sweats. An infection of the mouth called **thrush** may also appear. This produces a white coating on the tongue. Unusually severe forms of common skin conditions like dandruff, athlete's foot, and ringworm may also occur.

These are only a few of the common indicators of HIV infection. Just because someone has one or several of these symptoms does not mean that she or he is infected with HIV. These are also not the only symptoms. And just because a person doesn't show any symptoms doesn't mean that he or she can't be infected. Even if a person does not have any symptoms of being infected and seems completely healthy, that person is still capable of transmitting the virus to others. That is why, if someone has participated in any of the activities that can expose a person to the AIDS virus, it is very important that she or he be tested for the AIDS virus *before* any symptoms appear.

16.
Are the symptoms of HIV infection the same for women and men?

In general, the symptoms of HIV infection are the same for both men and women. However, women who are infected with HIV may experience an increased number of **yeast infections**, vaginal infections accompanied by a whitish discharge. Yeast infections are common, so a woman who has one should not immediately worry that she is infected. However, if a woman is having many outbreaks of yeast infections for no apparent reason, it might be a symptom of HIV infection and should be checked out.

Another indicator of HIV infection in women is **pelvic inflammatory disease**, or PID. This is an infection that causes swelling and soreness in the groin area. Again, PID can be a result of infections other than HIV infection, so it should not be assumed that a woman with PID is infected with the AIDS virus. But it can be a symptom and should be checked out, especially if it occurs frequently.

In the first years of the AIDS epidemic, it was thought that AIDS only affected men, so most of the early studies of the disease did not include studies of women. Because of this, we do not know exactly how or if AIDS affects women differently than it does men. Studies on women and HIV infection are relatively new, so it will take more years of research before we know more about how the disease affects women.

17.

What is the difference between being HIV-positive and having full-blown AIDS?

Being HIV-positive simply means that the body has been invaded by the AIDS virus. Just because a person is HIV-positive does not mean that he or she is sick. A person can be HIV-positive for many years before developing any serious infections. A person is said to have **full-blown AIDS** when she or he meets certain requirements established by the Centers for Disease Control. In general, a person has to test positive for antibodies to the AIDS virus (be HIV-positive, or seropositive) and have been severely affected by one or more of various opportunistic infections or cancers recognized by the CDC as resulting from immunosuppression. The opportunistic infections and cancers used by the CDC to diagnose full-blown AIDS are also called **indicator diseases**, because they show, or indicate, that a person has AIDS.

18.
Why is the CDC definition of full-blown AIDS so important?

The CDC definition of full-blown AIDS is used by many service organizations and insurance companies to determine whether or not a person receives benefits. Although they do not legally have to follow the CDC definition, some insurance companies and agencies such as Social Security use the CDC definition when accepting or rejecting medical claims or applications for disability. People who are HIV-positive (the first part of the CDC definition of having full-blown AIDS) but who have not yet developed an indicator disease (the second part of the definition) are not classified as having AIDS, and they may be turned down for benefits or their insurance companies may not cover all their expenses.

The CDC definition is important for another reason. The numbers reported by the CDC affect the way the government and people in general view the AIDS crisis. Because the CDC counts only those people officially classified as having full-blown AIDS, many people do not realize how widespread the AIDS crisis is. They do not see the millions of people currently infected with HIV who may develop full-blown AIDS in the future. And, because the CDC does not include on their list of indicator diseases infections that women get, a large number of women with AIDS are never counted. Until people begin to see how many people are really affected by HIV and AIDS, government funding and concern will continue to be inadequate.

The CDC definition of full-blown AIDS is a complicated and controversial issue, and different people and groups have different opinions about it. Some groups, such as ACT UP, have been fighting for changes in the CDC definition for a long time and have recently succeeded in getting the CDC to rethink their definition. But how the definition will change, and how it will affect the AIDS crisis, remains to be seen.

19.

How long after being infected with HIV does full-blown AIDS develop?

That depends on the person who is infected and how quickly the virus breaks down his or her immune system. Some people have been infected for over ten years without developing any major infections or complications. Others develop full-blown AIDS within a year or two of becoming infected. In general, it appears that about 30% of HIV-positive people develop an AIDS indicator disease within the first five years after testing positive, and 50% within nine years.

20.

Does everyone infected with HIV develop full-blown AIDS?

AIDS is a relatively new disease, and we have been studying it for only a little over ten years. Because of the long **incubation period** that AIDS has, no one is absolutely certain what percentage of people infected with HIV will actually develop full-blown AIDS. Until more time has gone by and researchers have had time to monitor the progress of people infected with HIV in recent years, we won't have any final answers. What is important to remember is that, even if an HIV-positive person *never* develops AIDS, he or she will *always* have the AIDS virus in his or her system for as long as he or she lives and will *always* be able to transmit the virus to other people.

21.

How many people have AIDS?

At the end of 1991, there were 206,392 reported cases of people with full-blown AIDS in the United States. This may not seem like a lot of people, but when you look at the history of the AIDS epidemic, the numbers are very dramatic. The first five cases of AIDS were reported in June 1981. Between 1981 and August 1989, 100,000 cases of AIDS were reported. That is a span of eight years. Then, between August 1989 and December 1991, a span of only a little over two years, another 100,000 cases were reported. What this tells us is that the number of people infected in

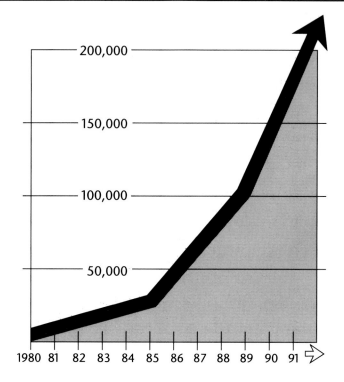

the early 1980s who are just now developing full-blown AIDS is very high. By 1993, the number of cases of people with full-blown AIDS is expected to be over 400,000.

22.
How many young people have AIDS?

By the end of 1991, 789 people between the ages of 13 and 19 had been diagnosed with full-blown AIDS. An additional 8,160 people between the ages of 20 and 24 also had AIDS. AIDS is the sixth leading cause of death in people 15–24, and the third leading cause in people 25–44.

These numbers may not seem very large. After all, 789 people could probably make up the attendance at a single football game at a big high school. But what is frightening is the rapid growth of AIDS among young people. In the last few years, the number of people under the age of 19 diagnosed with full-blown AIDS has doubled every 14 months. If the disease continues at this rate, there will be almost 13,000 teenagers with AIDS by the end of 1995.

The AIDS epidemic seems to be affecting some groups of young people more severely than others. Young women are being hit particularly hard. Between 1989 and 1990, there was a 49% increase in the number of AIDS cases in girls 13–19 reported to the CDC. In New York and New Jersey, AIDS is now the leading cause of death among adolescent African-American and Hispanic women.

Two other groups showing a sharp increase in AIDS cases are homeless young people and **bisexual** and **gay** male teenagers. In a recent study, it was estimated that as many as 25% of all homeless teenagers might be HIV-positive. And while the number of adult gay and bisexual men becoming infected with the AIDS virus has decreased every year, the number of gay and bisexual men between 13 and 19 becoming infected has actually *increased*. There are many reasons for this, the greatest of which is that there are very few places where gay and bisexual teens can go to talk about AIDS issues. As a result, many young people still deny that they are at risk for becoming infected with the AIDS virus. Fortunately, centers are being established especially for both homeless teens and gay teens. For listings of these groups, look in the Resource Guide at the back of this book.

23.
How do we know how many people in the United States have AIDS?

Whenever a person in the United States is diagnosed as having full-blown AIDS, this information is sent to the Centers for Disease Control. This is how we know approximately how many people with AIDS there are in the United States. This should not be confused with people who test positive for HIV. While some states do report the total number of known cases of HIV-infection, most do not. So if you go to a clinic and have a test for the AIDS virus, this information is most likely not reported to the CDC, even if the test is positive. That is why statistics for the number of people infected with HIV can only be estimated. The number of people with AIDS in the United States is also higher than the CDC numbers show because there are many people who have AIDS who have never gone to a doctor and who have never been counted, either because they are scared, cannot afford to go to a doctor, or because they simply do not know anything about AIDS. This number also does not include the large number of homeless people estimated to have AIDS.

24.
Do all people with AIDS die?

Because AIDS has really only been studied for a little over ten years, we cannot say if all people diagnosed with full-blown AIDS will die. What we do know is that of the 202,921 cases of full-blown AIDS in people over 13 years old reported since 1981, 131,383, or about 65%, have died. Of the 3,471 cases of AIDS reported in people under 13 years old, 1,850, or about 53%, have died. Three out of four, or 75%, of people who develop full-blown AIDS die within three years.

Because AIDS information is becoming more readily available, people are getting tested sooner and starting treatment sooner. And as new treatments are developed, people with AIDS will live longer and healthier lives. Until another ten years goes by, we will not know how this is affecting the percentage of people who die from AIDS.

25.
How did AIDS start?

No one is sure how AIDS started. The first cases of what is now called AIDS were diagnosed in 1981 on the West Coast of the United States. At that time, it was thought that it was a disease that would only affect a few people. Some people believed it might even go away. But as the years went on, AIDS began to spread all across the country, touching every segment of the population.

Some researchers believe that the virus originated in central Africa, where many people are now infected, but no one can really say where the virus came from originally. While there are many theories about where AIDS originated, it is more important now to find a cure for the disease than it is to worry about where it came from.

26.
Is AIDS a problem in other countries?

AIDS is a worldwide problem. At the end of 1991, the World Health Organization reported 447,494 cases of AIDS worldwide, including 252,977 in North and South America, 129,066 in Africa, 60,195 in Europe, 2,813 in Australia and New Zealand, and 1,254 in Asia. These numbers are probably very low in relation to the number of people in these areas who actually have AIDS, however, because many countries do not have adequate facilities for diagnosing or tracking people with AIDS.

27.
Is there a vaccine for AIDS?

Right now there is no **vaccine** for AIDS. This means that you cannot get a shot to protect yourself from the AIDS virus like you can for measles or polio. Because AIDS has only been studied for about ten years, we do not know everything about the disease. Also, the AIDS virus differs from person to person. Because of this, it is very difficult to manufacture a vaccine that would work on everyone. Even within one person, the virus is able to change its structure over time, so a vaccine that might help one day might not be useful the next. Scientists are working to develop a vaccine for HIV, but it is doubtful that an effective vaccine will be available for at least five to ten years.

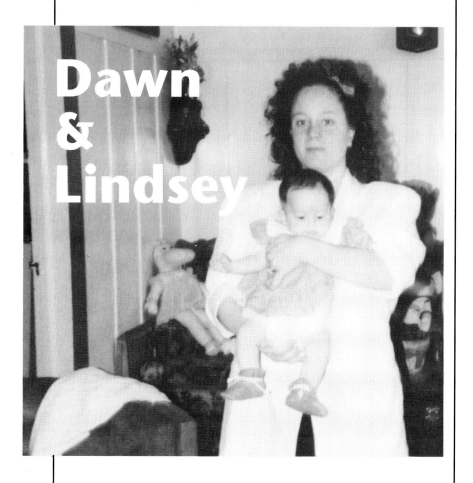

In 1987, at the age of 21, all of Dawn Marcal's dreams had come true. She had gone to college, worked at a job she liked, was married to a wonderful man, and had a stepson she adored. And, after months of trying to get pregnant, she had a baby. A beautiful, happy little girl whose smile and laughter made everyone around her feel better, Lindsey was everything

that Dawn had ever wanted. She spent all her time with her daughter, enjoying everything about being a new mother. As Dawn says, "Lindsey would burp and I thought it was a miracle."

After three months of what Dawn calls "normal babyhood—breast-feeding and sleepless nights and dirty diapers and learning to be a mommy," she noticed that Lindsey would turn blue around the mouth whenever she would cry. She rushed her daughter to the emergency room three times, only to be told each time that Lindsey was fine.

Then, while Lindsey was getting her first round of baby shots, the doctor giving the shots also saw that Lindsey was turning blue when she cried. He put her in the hospital and diagnosed her as having viral pneumonia, an infection of the lungs. Since Dawn had had a difficult delivery and Lindsey had swallowed some fluid during her birth, the doctors thought the pneumonia might be a result of that.

But Lindsey had another virus in her lungs, one that the doctors couldn't identify. Test after test failed to determine what it was that was making the little girl so sick. Finally they let Lindsey go home.

After another month, Lindsey still wasn't getting any better. She was not gaining weight or developing as quickly as she should, so the doctors put her back in the hospital. This time, they asked Dawn if she had ever done anything that might have put her at risk for contracting the AIDS virus. In her teens, Dawn had injected intravenous drugs and had had unprotected sex with a man who also did drugs. But that was years before, and she felt fine.

Just to make sure, in November of 1987 Dawn went for the HIV test. It came back positive. Her husband, Henry, was also tested. His test was negative. Then they had Lindsey tested. Like Dawn, she was positive for the AIDS virus. Because babies sometimes outgrow diseases that they inherit from their mothers as they develop their own immune systems, Dawn hoped that Lindsey would lose the virus that she had passed on. But she didn't, and when Lindsey was one year old, she was diagnosed as having full-blown AIDS.

Dawn and Henry did everything they could think of to help Lindsey get better. They enrolled her in experimental drug treatment programs, took her to doctors specializing in herbal healing, and tried nutritional programs. They even took her to a priest who was said to be able to heal people.

Nothing worked, and when Lindsey was only 18 months old she died. Since then, Dawn has been traveling around the country telling young people about AIDS. She has also been fighting her own battle with the disease, a battle she has been winning for almost nine years.

You tested positive in 1987. Do you know when you were infected?

I was infected in 1983, when I was 17. The odds are I got the virus from intravenous drug use. But the same guy I shared needles with I slept with without using a condom, so it could have been that too.

Did you know about AIDS when you were 17?

No. You didn't hear anything. All you knew about birth control was you take a pill and you're safe. I had some sex education in school. They told me about birth control pills, they told me about condoms, they told me about sexually transmitted diseases. But nobody said anything about AIDS.

When you started hearing about AIDS, did you think that you might be infected?

No. What I actually thought was boy, was I lucky. Was I lucky I didn't have that.

What's been the biggest change in your life since testing positive?

I have a different perception than a lot of people because I had a baby. When she was diagnosed the worst thing that could happen to me had already happened to me— the fact that I would let my daughter die, that I would watch her die. Watching her living and dying just 100% turned my life around.

It sounds like when your daughter was alive you kept on going for her. Now who do you keep on for?

I keep on for me, but it took me a long time to get to this point. My daughter was everything. She was my whole life. You just can't comprehend that unless you have a child. And I guess being a mom is even more special. I never thought about myself. If I remembered to take my medication while she was alive I was lucky. And then she died and I spent a year or more—we're talking heavy grief—crying every second of the day. And then that starts to ease up and you have to make a switch from her to you. I spent the first two years after she died validating her life. I wasn't even thinking about me. The people I worked with used to say, "Stop talking about the baby all the time. Tell people something about you, tell them what you feel, what it's doing to you." It took me a long time to make that switch.

Does AIDS make you refocus your life?
It cuts out all the crap. When you're sick you don't care who cleans you up, you don't care if somebody sees you with your breast hanging out. All you care about is not being in pain anymore and being able to live and not give up and not die at that point. It cuts close to everything. It doesn't matter if you don't have a pretty baby or a mansion or even an old television. None of this material stuff means anything anymore. For me life became real simple: This doesn't make me sick, so I will do this; this gives me pain, so forget it.

Is that what everything comes down to?
Yeah, it really can. For instance, every day I'm grateful that I can taste my food today and I can breathe today and I can walk to the store by myself if I want to. In March I was real sick. I lost my hair and I dropped 55 pounds in two weeks. I was in the hospital for a while and then in bed at home for a couple of months, and my parents would come over and they'd cook for me and force me to eat. They live across the street, so they wanted me to come to their house during the day so I'd get a change of scenery. But I would scream and cry all the way across the street. I would cry and cry and sob because it was extremely painful to try to walk. Such an

effort. Everything was such an effort. When you're better you try to be really grateful for it and acknowledge it. Not to take it for granted.

Has your family always been supportive?
Yeah, my family's great. We've always been close. They knew when I went for the test. They knew I had done drugs. They knew all about my past. They were always really supportive and understanding, and they still are.

How about your husband? How does he take all this?
He's real good. He doesn't think about the future so much. He kind of stays in the moment, which is something that's good. He closes right up if I get too emotional, closes right down because he doesn't know how to make my pain stop. He cannot bear it. He cannot bear to see my pain. I've hated him at times for that. We can talk about AIDS. We can talk about anything except how much I miss my daughter and how much that breaks my heart every day. He can't deal with any of that because he misses her too.

Do you ever feel like you've been cheated out of time?
There is a certain pressure to feel like that. Sometimes I see old couples and I know that that could be me and my husband, because I really believe that we have a relationship that will last, which is very rare nowadays. But now, who knows?

Do you resent people who have more time?

Oh God, no. I have no resentment or bitterness on any subject, not even for the guy who gave this to me. I don't have any of that because all that stuff will kill you. My biggest thing is sad. I feel sad. I look at those old couples and think, "I won't get to that point." Or maybe I will. My doctors have told me that I'm a miracle anyway because they haven't figured out why I haven't died yet.

Do you ever forget about what happened to Lindsey?

No, never. For instance, we went to Hawaii and had a really good time, my husband and my son and me. We were sitting at a table one day, and it was a table for four, and the seat next to me was empty and I knew it should be for Lindsey. There should be a little girl there. And sometimes I lose it at whatever moment. Then I start crying really bad and I have to control myself. It's what I call the Big Ones, when you're going to open your mouth and start screaming and sobbing at the top of your lungs. That's happened a couple of times. You never forget. You cannot. It's part of every moment. That doesn't mean I don't have a good time. It doesn't mean I don't laugh and play and smile, because those things I learned from my daughter and I do them. One of the biggest changes is that you try so hard not to take anything for granted. Nothing. You don't know if you have tomorrow. You don't know if you have an hour from now.

Do you blame yourself for Lindsey's death?

Sometimes, of course. But when I first started getting into the guilt stuff my husband said, "No, you're not going to do it." At first I really felt I deserved whatever happened to me. But I don't think that's the way it is anymore. I did everything I could to save her, I did everything I could. Angerness and bitterness and all that stuff, all that will do is eat you up. It wasn't going to save my daughter's life, it wasn't going to make it any easier on her. You grow so much and you learn so much that you go beyond any of that.

What do you wish you knew nine years ago?

I wish I knew about self-respect. And I wish someone had taught me about real life in school. I needed to know how to use a condom to protect myself a lot more than I needed calculus.

What do you think young people need to know most?

They need to learn to love themselves. Because if you love yourself and you like who you are you're not going to stick that needle in your arm. You're not going to let someone have unsafe sex with you. Many times when I speak, I'm the first person who ever tells these kids that it's really important that they take care of themselves, that they're worthy of love no matter what they've done or what mistakes they've made. We don't teach kids that. What you learn from society is that you have to have nice cars, you have to have a model body and if you don't you're not good enough. I always tell kids, "Don't wait for your parents or anyone else to love you the way you want to be loved. You ought to do it for yourself. Start with you."

That was the way it was for me. Life was so crummy and I was hurting so much I could never see it being happy or anything. I thought I wouldn't care what happened in a couple years or even a couple days. But then you change. You grow up, your situation changes, your life changes and suddenly life can be a beautiful, wonderful place to be. If anybody had told me that when I was a teenager it would have been gold to me.

I found this wonderful man who I actually trusted. I never thought I would. I had a wonderful little boy and my own baby that meant everything to me. And then the past came along and wiped it all out. So I tell the kids that you really have to be conscious about the choices you are making now, because if I had made different choices for myself, my daughter would be alive today, and that's something I have to live with every second of my life.

You can say "don't do drugs" and "don't have sex," but that's not enough. With kids we need to be honest. Talk about anal sex and IV drugs use. Teach them how to clean needles. Be open with our kids, because what are we protecting them from? What are we hiding from them? Nothing but ignorance is going to kill them in the end.

Is the self-esteem issue different for girls?

It's very much different. I see this all the time. I thought my whole self-worth was wrapped up in if I had a boyfriend or not. And if a guy didn't like me, then there was something wrong with me, not something wrong with the guy. When I was a teenager the one thing that I really wanted to do was to find some wonderful guy and fall madly in love and have a great romantic relationship, and the big mistake I made was that I believed it when some guy would say to me, "Hey, Dawn, if we had sex that would bring us closer together. That would make our relationship even stronger." That's a very common way of thinking for young girls. It took me a while to figure out that somebody wasn't going to love me just because I slept with them. I got hurt a lot, so I decided that I was going to build this big wall around myself and nobody was going to know how much I was hurting and I was going to pretend like I didn't know how much I was hurting inside. I did all kinds of really crazy things, really destructive things. I tried all kinds of drugs and alcohol. I didn't like who I was. I guess I didn't think I was pretty enough or smart enough or whatever and I wasn't a virgin, so I thought I ruined my entire life because I wasn't a virgin, and it didn't matter if somebody hurt me or if I hurt myself.

Do you think about dying?

When I get sick, I really think about it. When you've been real sick you get to a point where you say, "This is what's going to happen. Just stop the pain because I can't deal with it anymore." You come to that point because it's too much. And you get really tired living with that kind of anxiety and fear. Sometimes during your illness you accept death as a possibility and think, "Boy, am I stupid to fight it the whole way." You know how you're going to die, and you know that it will probably be a lot bigger than you would have wanted.

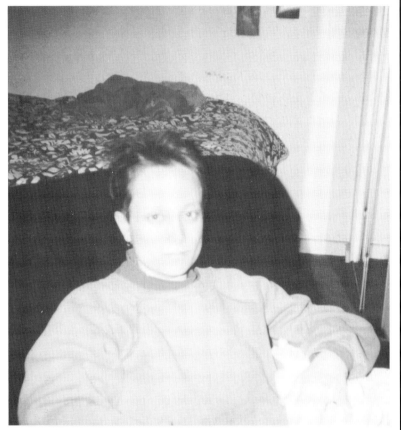

Dawn in 1991

How has that changed the way you live?

I don't know when I'm going to die. Maybe I'll live a long time, maybe there will be a cure. Who knows? But while I'm here I'm going to have the best time I can. I know that me, my family, and everyone who's been affected by my having AIDS, we've grown so much more over the last three or four years than we would have if I hadn't had it. Nobody really knows how much time they have, and what I really want to do is shake them up. Because what is really important? What's important when you're holding your sick baby in your arms and you want to do everything you can to make her better? Not a Mercedes. Most people are so materialistic that they lose sight of what this world can teach us. You don't know until you've been through something like this. You just don't know.

FACT

&

FICTION

28.
Can I get AIDS from toilet seats or silverware or from shaking hands or kissing a person with AIDS?

The biggest myth about AIDS is that it is easy to get. Unlike other viruses, the AIDS virus cannot live in air, food, or water. You cannot contract HIV from swimming in a pool with someone with HIV or from sharing food or a drink with an infected person. You cannot get HIV from using the same bathroom or using the same silverware as a person with AIDS. You cannot get HIV from shaking someone's hand, talking to that person, or kissing him or her. The virus has to come into direct contact with your bloodstream in order to infect you, and this can happen almost exclusively through sexual intercourse, sharing infected needles or syringes, or receiving infected blood products or a blood transfusion.

29.
Don't only people in certain "risk groups" get AIDS?

In the first few years of the AIDS epidemic, it seemed that only a few certain groups were acquiring the AIDS virus. It was incorrectly assumed that only those in these so-called risk groups could be infected with HIV. People who did not consider themselves part of these groups thought that they could never get AIDS.

Today, we know that HIV affects *everyone* regardless of age, gender, sexual preference, or race. There is no longer any such thing as a risk group because we all can be at risk for becoming infected with HIV. Instead, we now say that there are certain **high-risk behaviors**. A high-risk behavior is any behavior that puts your bloodstream in contact with any of the bodily fluids that can transmit the AIDS virus. This includes sharing needles when injecting intravenous drugs (including steroids) and having **unprotected** vaginal, anal, or oral sex.

30.
My friend is gay, and I've heard that a lot of homosexuals get AIDS. Should I worry that he has AIDS?

Many people think that all gay, or **homosexual**, people are infected with HIV because when the AIDS epidemic first began, the largest number of people with HIV infection were gay and bisexual men. Because of this, many people mistakenly thought AIDS was a "gay disease" and assumed that *all* homosexuals had AIDS. During the last ten years, however, the gay and **lesbian** community has done a remarkable job of educating people, both homosexual and **heterosexual**, about HIV and AIDS. As a result, the number of newly infected gay men has decreased dramatically. Lesbians who don't use intravenous drugs have always been the group with the lowest rate of infection. Just because someone is gay does not mean that she or he is more likely to get AIDS then anyone else. AIDS affects everyone. In fact, about 90% of all the new AIDS cases reported to the CDC have been diagnosed in heterosexual men and women.

These statistics are not the same, however, for gay men under the age of 19. While the number of adult gay men newly diagnosed with HIV has gone down dramatically, the number of teenage men diagnosed has gone up. This still does not mean that you have to worry about a friend just because that person is gay or bisexual. AIDS cases in teenagers in *all* categories is increasing, and anyone who participates in any high-risk behavior is at risk for contracting HIV.

31.
Isn't AIDS a problem only in big cities, like New York and San Francisco?

It may seem like AIDS only affects people in large cities, but this is only because there are more people in cities than there are in smaller towns. In fact, statistics show that the number of AIDS cases diagnosed in rural areas is increasing dramatically. This is due in part to the fact that, even though AIDS information is becoming more available, many people in areas outside of big cities still think that they don't have to worry about the disease.

32.
Can a person be born with AIDS?

A baby can be born infected with HIV if the mother is infected. Because a **fetus** shares a blood supply with its mother, a pregnant HIV-positive woman has a 30% chance of passing the virus on to her unborn baby. Even if a baby has not actually contracted the AIDS virus, the antibodies to the virus will be present in his or her blood at birth. These antibodies were produced by the infected mother's body and passed to the baby before birth. While they are present, the baby's blood will test positive for HIV. In most cases, these antibodies are broken down over a period of several months, and the baby will then test negative.

33.
Can an infected woman pass the virus to her baby through breast-feeding even if the baby is born without the virus?

During breast-feeding, any antibodies in a woman's bloodstream may be passed to her baby through her breast milk. This also means that any viruses in the bloodstream can also be passed on, including the AIDS virus. If a baby ingests the breast milk of a woman infected with HIV, the baby may also be taking in the virus that is in her bloodstream.

34.
Can the AIDS virus pass through the skin?

HIV cannot pass through unbroken skin. The virus must have direct access to the bloodstream in order to enter the body. You will not contract the AIDS virus if someone with AIDS spits, bleeds, vomits, or cries on you, or if your unbroken skin comes into contact with their urine, feces, semen, vaginal secretions, or breast milk. You cannot get AIDS from changing the diaper of a baby infected with HIV or from handling the dirty clothes of someone with AIDS, as long as your skin is unbroken.

The virus can, however, enter the body if there are any cuts or open sores present, because these offer an entrance for the virus into the bloodstream. Because of this, people who care for people with HIV infection may wear protective rubber gloves when handling diapers, bandages, or clothes that are heavily soiled with infected bodily fluids. Also, the moist mucous membranes that line the mouth, rectum, eyes, nose, and vagina are less resistant, and it is possible that the AIDS virus could pass through them if they come into direct contact with it.

35.
Someone at my school has AIDS.
Should I be afraid to talk to her?

You should not be afraid to talk to, hug, kiss, or touch someone infected with HIV. People with HIV are no different than people with any other transmissible disease, and casual contact with them will not put you in any danger. Unless you are having unprotected sex or sharing needles with an infected person, you are not at risk for becoming infected by him or her.

There have been several cases in which people have tried to ban infected children from attending public schools or have removed their children from school when an infected child was allowed to attend. These people simply did not have the facts about AIDS and were acting out of fear. Attending school is actually more risky for an HIV-infected person—she or he could easily catch a disease from another student or teacher because of the way immunosuppression lowers the body's resistance.

36.

What if someone with the virus coughs or sneezes near me?

You don't have to worry about people with HIV coughing or sneezing near you. They have to worry about *you* coughing or sneezing near them. You cannot become infected with HIV simply by breathing the virus in, so it cannot be spread through sneezing or coughing like a cold virus can. But if you have a cold or flu or other virus, and you sneeze near someone infected with HIV, that person can catch whatever you have. And because the immune system is weakened, catching a cold or flu isn't just inconvenient, it can be deadly. An infection that a healthy person can easily fight off will further weaken an infected person's suppressed immune system and may lead to serious complications and even death.

37.

My friends say that you can't get AIDS the first time you have sex. Is this true?

It is interesting that some of the same myths that people used to believe about getting pregnant are now being believed about contracting the AIDS virus. It is possible to become infected with HIV through only one exposure, just as it can take only one instance of sexual intercourse to become pregnant. As long as you are participating in risky behavior, you are risking contracting HIV. It doesn't matter if it is the first time you are participating in the behavior or the thousandth.

38.
Can I get AIDS from my doctor or dentist?

Not if your doctor or dentist takes the proper precautions when performing any **invasive procedures**. An invasive procedure is anything, like a dental cleaning or an incision, that results in direct contact with a person's blood. There have been several cases in which people claimed to have been infected by a dentist, but it is believed that in these cases the dentist either used instruments that were infected with the blood of a previous patient and had not been cleaned properly or had cuts on her or his hands and did not wear gloves to protect the patient. If all instruments used in an invasive procedure are cleaned thoroughly, and if the doctor or dentist wears protective gloves, there is virtually no risk of contracting the AIDS virus.

A doctor or dentist actually has to worry more about contracting HIV from an infected patient than the patient does about contracting it from the doctor or dentist. Doctors and dentists often come into direct contact with blood and other bodily fluids. If the dentist or doctor has cuts on his or her hands and does not wear protective gloves, then there is the possibility that he or she could contract the AIDS virus if a patient's infected bodily fluids come into contact with the cuts.

If you are concerned about the possibility of contracting HIV from your doctor or dentist, it might be a good idea to discuss the issue with her or him. Ask what precautions he or she uses to protect *both* of you from HIV infection.

39.
What is the risk of getting AIDS from a blood transfusion or organ transplant?

In the early 1980s, some people became infected with HIV by receiving infected blood in **transfusions**. Many of these people were **hemophiliacs**, males with an inherited blood condition who require frequent transfusions of blood products to help their blood clot effectively. Some people were also infected when they received infected blood during transfusions as parts of operations or when they received organ transplants from infected people.

In 1985 the American Red Cross began screening all donated blood for HIV. They also asked people who had participated in high-risk behavior not to donate blood. As another safety measure, all donated organs are now tested for HIV. As a result, the donated blood supply in the United States is very safe. The chance of becoming infected with HIV through a transfusion or through an organ transplant today is about 1 in 40,000, less than your chance of dying from the flu or being killed in a car accident, which is 1 in 5,000.

40.
Can I get AIDS from donating blood?

There is a big difference between donating blood and receiving blood through a transfusion. When you donate blood you are having blood taken out of your own body. The needle used is a new one, and it is never reused. It is thrown away as soon as the blood is drawn. The only blood you are coming into contact with is your own. You can't catch anything that you don't already have, including AIDS, from donating blood.

41.
Can I get AIDS from performing CPR on someone with AIDS?

When performing CPR (**cardiopulmonary resuscitation**) or other mouth-to-mouth life-saving techniques on a person, you do come into contact with that person's saliva. While the AIDS virus has been found in saliva, there is not enough of it to transmit AIDS to someone. However, lifeguards, paramedics, police officers, and firefighters do often wear protective masks when performing CPR in case there is any blood present in the victim's mouth, since HIV is found in blood.

42.
Can mosquitoes, ticks, or other biting insects transmit the virus?

Mosquitoes, ticks, and other insects that suck blood are not capable of transmitting the AIDS virus. Mosquitoes and ticks can only take blood *out* of someone's body; they are not able to inject it back *into* someone. If they did suck blood from an infected person, they could not then put that blood back into someone else. Even if they were capable of injecting blood, the amount of blood removed by a mosquito or tick is not enough to contain sufficient quantities of the virus to infect anyone.

AIDS also cannot be transmitted or contracted by animals. While there is a virus similar to AIDS that causes immunodeficiency in monkeys, it is not the same as HIV. It is not possible to get AIDS from a dog, cat, or any other animal.

43.
Can I contract the AIDS virus by having my ears pierced or getting a tattoo?

Since the needle used to pierce ears does come into contact with blood, it is possible to become infected with HIV if the needle used to pierce your ears was used on someone infected with HIV and the needle was not cleaned and sterilized properly afterward. Most places that pierce ears, however, clean their equipment with alcohol before each use, so the risk of contracting the virus this way is very small.

In tattooing, a small needle is injected into the skin many times to form a design. This needle comes into contact with blood, which can remain in and on the needle. If an infected needle is then used to make a tattoo on someone else, that person could become infected by the contaminated blood. If you are getting a tattoo, make sure that the person making the tattoo uses a brand-new needle and not one that has already been used on someone else.

44.
I can always tell if someone is infected, can't I?

Unless the person is very far along with an AIDS-related condition, you probably can't. People infected with HIV look just like everyone else. Some people think that everyone with AIDS is very thin, balding, and covered in sores. This is not true. Some people in the last stages of AIDS do look like this, but the majority of people infected with HIV look completely healthy.

45.
Married people don't get AIDS, do they?

Anyone can get AIDS, and this includes married people or people who have been with the same person for a long time. You never know what your partner did before you were together, and your partner may not even be aware that she or he has participated in any high-risk behavior. Remember, the AIDS virus can be present in the body for as long as ten years before any symptoms of infection begin to show. There is also the chance that the person you are with is participating in high-risk behavior with someone else and you don't know it.

This does not mean that you should be suspicious of your partner or demand that he or she take an HIV antibody test; it just means that you should not assume that just because you have been with someone for a while that you are immune to AIDS. Of course, the risk of becoming infected with the AIDS virus increases with the number of different sexual partners a person has. If you are in a relationship with only one person, you and your partner may both want to take an HIV-antibody test. Even if you don't, it is a good idea to discuss the issue of HIV and AIDS with you partner. This gives you the opportunity to ask each other any questions you might have.

46.
Can people with HIV infection still have sex?

Just because someone is infected with HIV does not mean that he or she must stop having sex. What it does mean is that people infected with HIV have to properly use a condom every time they have oral, vaginal, or anal sex. They must also make sure that they tell anyone that they are having sex with that they are infected. Some people believe that as long as they are using condoms and taking the recommended precautions, they don't have to tell their partners that they are infected. This is not true. Condoms can break or be defective, so even though using condoms reduces the risk of transmission, there is still some risk. If you are infected with HIV, it is your responsibility to let potential sexual partners know this before engaging in any kind of sexual behavior.

47.

Isn't it dangerous to have people with HIV on a sports team?

Because playing sports often involves coming into contact with another person's sweat, and possibly blood, some people are concerned that they may be putting themselves at risk by playing sports with someone with HIV. But while the AIDS virus may possibly be found in the sweat of some individuals with HIV infection, it is in such small amounts that it poses little, if any, risk to other athletes. And while loss of blood does sometimes occur during rough sports, the possibility of contracting HIV by getting infected blood on your unbroken skin is very slight and really is not an issue where sports are concerned.

Peter

Photo: Freddy Rodrigues

In 1989, as a 17-year-old high school student, Peter Zamora donated blood during an American Red Cross blood drive. A month and a half later, he received a letter stating that one of the tests that was done as part of the screening process for all donated blood had come back positive. He threw the letter away. Peter also threw away the next seven letters the Red Cross mailed him.

Later in the year, Peter began a new relationship, and he and his lover both decided to be tested for the AIDS virus. On November 9, Peter went to his doctor's office for his test results and found out he was HIV-positive. Today, at 20, Peter is a well-known AIDS educator and activist working with Body Positive of Miami. He travels around the country speaking to groups about HIV and AIDS and telling his story.

Why didn't you answer the letters from the Red Cross?

When I got the first letter, I had an idea of what it might be. There was always the thought in my mind that I might be HIV-positive. I just didn't want to confront it. Then, when I met my lover and we started getting serious, I had to confront it.

How did you react when you first got your results?

Shock. There was a coldness, a numbness, all over my body. Then there was disbelief. The nurse who told me asked if I was all right and I just looked at her and said, "Sure. What's next?" She said, "It might not hit you today, but it might hit you tomorrow or the day after. Then you are going to need some help." I thanked her and left. I walked out of the office, and on the way to the car I just broke down. All of these questions raced through my mind. Was I going to die? Would I be able to finish high school? Could they fire me from work? How was I going to tell people? What if I got sick? All these questions that I needed answers to. Then I got in the car and let it out. I drove to my lover's house, went inside, and went to sleep.

How did your lover react to your testing positive?
He called to see how I was, and he asked if I had gotten my test results back. I said that I had, and that I was HIV-positive. There was this brief silence, and then he asked me if I wanted him to come home. I told him that I would rather be alone, and I went back to sleep.

Did you tell your family?
The day I found out was my sister's birthday, of all days. She called me to remind me that there was going to be a birthday dinner for her that night. I tried to get myself out of it, but she wanted me there, and I knew it meant a lot to her. I had to go and sit through the dinner and smile and laugh. Then, about a week later, I told them.

How did they respond?
When I told my sister, the first thing that came out of her was, "What do I have to do to protect my little girls?" That was a very real concern for her then. I had to explain to her that no one could get it from being around me or drinking out of my cup or anything. Once we got past that, then we got down to crying, and she said that she would help me do whatever I had to do.

When I told my father, I said, "I am HIV-positive." He said, "What's that?" I explained to him that HIV is the virus that causes AIDS. Then he wanted to know if I had AIDS. I had to sit down and explain to him the difference between HIV and AIDS and what it all meant. Before we were able to cry and they could say that they would do anything they could for me, I had to educate them. And that was tough.

Because you were educating yourself at the same time?

I didn't know anything about HIV and AIDS. Like most kids, I had the facts and myths confused in my mind. All the information I had was mixed up, and no one sat me down and gave me clear answers.

I knew that AIDS was out there, but it wasn't real for me. It wasn't my disease. I remember one Saturday in 1986 turning on the television and seeing Ryan White, the young hemophiliac who died of AIDS not long ago. At that time, Ryan was speaking in schools, and I remember thinking how brave he was. But I still didn't connect AIDS with myself. I thought it was a disease of older gay men, hemophiliacs, drug addicts, and prostitutes, and I didn't link myself with those groups. I was an honor student, I ran 10 miles a day, I was basically a good kid. So, when I tested positive, what I knew about AIDS was that it was a disease of bad people, of dirty people, and that once you got AIDS, you were going to die. That's all I knew about AIDS.

Do you know when you were infected?

It could have happened any time from age 14 on. I don't know who infected me. I do know it was from unprotected sex.

How has life changed the most since you tested positive?

It's changed the most in my awareness of who I am. AIDS made me stop what I was doing and start to think about what I wanted, what I was doing to get it, what I could do differently, and who I am. AIDS has basically changed the way I see the whole world—the way I see myself, the way I see relationships, the way I see my family, the way I see life, the way I see death. AIDS has changed a lot of things for the better.

When you first tested positive, did you think your life was over?

I thought I was going to die. I even graduated a year early from high school because I didn't think I would have enough time to finish. I was an honor student, and I used my extra credits to skip my senior year. I didn't tell anybody why I did it. I just said I wanted to go to college. Everybody thought it went along with the kind of person I was.

You didn't tell any of your friends that you were positive?

I told my best friend. But nobody else.

How did it feel, not being able to talk to anyone?

At that time it was okay, because I still didn't want to talk about it. I was in denial. I told my family, I told my lover at the time, I told my best friend, and that was it. I really didn't want to think or talk about it anymore.

Were you receiving any medical treatment?

At the time, I didn't really have to do much. I was HIV-positive, but my T-cell count was high—it still is—so there really wasn't anything I could do except exercise and keep to a balanced diet.

It wasn't until April of 1990, when I was hospitalized with shingles, that I started to deal with it. Up to then, I could admit that I was HIV-positive, but I didn't have to think about what that meant. When I started thinking about it, I would turn on the television, listen to the radio, pick up the telephone and call a friend, go dancing, go to a movie, anything to forget. But then I got shingles, and they were all over my face, right there in front of me. I couldn't ignore it anymore. Suddenly I had to face the fact that I was HIV-positive and that I could get sick and die. I had to deal with it.

How did you deal with it?

In the hospital I felt really lonely. It was incredible. My room was filled with people all the time because my whole family was there. With Cuban families, even if you're only in the hospital for tests, your whole family visits—grandmothers, cousins you haven't seen in three hundred years, everyone. So I was never alone. My room was filled with flowers and cards. Friends were calling me constantly. But I still felt very lonely because I felt like nobody understood what I was going through.

Another thing that happened at the hospital was that my anger came out. One of the reasons I think I felt so alone was that I didn't want to talk to my family about my anger or how lonely I was because I didn't want to make them feel bad.

How did you overcome that?
When I got out of the hospital, I went to my first support group. Up until that time, I believed that once you got AIDS you died. I had all the facts, but I still believed this. And, on a subconscious level, I still believed that people with AIDS were bad people, dirty people, or people who just weren't like me.

When I walked into my first support group, there were about 15 older gay men, a facilitator, and one woman. I was very frightened. I didn't want to talk to anybody. I sat back and listened. As we went around the room introducing ourselves, each person said things like, "My name is Frank. I have AIDS. I was diagnosed in 1985."

When it was time for the one woman in the group to speak, she looked at everybody in the room and said, "My name is Sonia Singleton and I am a person living with AIDS." And that really confused me, because I had never put the words *AIDS* and *living* together. As I watched Sonia speak to the whole group, I saw how proud she was, and how strong she was. She knew who she was and how she felt, and how anyone else felt about her didn't concern her.

I really felt a lot of admiration for her, and I knew I wanted to be exactly like her. I started going to the support group, and I got close to Sonia. She was the first person I really admired who got me to come out of my shell and start talking to people. Through her I met so many wonderful people who were living with AIDS, not dying of it. And I realized that if they could do it, I could do it too. Everybody around me was living with AIDS. They weren't talking about dying. They were talking about the fact that they were sick and had to go to a doctor, that they had to get medicine or whatever, but no one was talking about death. They were talking about living. That completely changed my view of what AIDS was.

Then you started speaking to other people about your experience?

On November 4, 1990, almost a year to the day after I found out I was positive, the first newspaper story about me came out. Then there was an avalanche effect. I haven't stopped talking since.

What keeps you going?

I'm not sure. I think sometimes it's anger, sometimes it's love. Sometimes it's just that I get out of bed and I'm so angry that I want to get up there and give everyone hell. Then other times I feel that people need to know what I have to say, and I tell them out of love. Other times I just feel lost, and there's nothing else to do except get up and talk about the fact that that day I feel a little bit lost and things don't have a hell of a lot of meaning.

And that's okay. What I've come to realize is that whatever emotion I happen to be feeling, I have the right to feel. I need to feel it and let go of it so that I have space for all the other emotions I need to feel.

Do you ever forget that you are positive?

Even in my happiest moments it's there. But that doesn't mean that it makes my happy moments any less happy. I have learned how to deal with being HIV-positive, and I know that I am a better person because I am HIV-positive. That doesn't mean that I'm always a positive person. I've just learned how to live with the disease. And it doesn't mean that every day I'm happy and it's a good day. Sometimes I get up and I'm very angry and I hate God and hate myself. Sometimes I hate the whole world and I want to die because the thought of living with AIDS is a lot scarier than the thought of dying from it.

How has testing positive changed your personal relationships?

I found out I was positive a month after I met my first lover. And he was good about it, he didn't let me go. But we didn't have a lot of communication. We didn't talk about our anger or our fears. And I was changing constantly. Every day I was learning something new about myself, about the world, about everything. Neither one of us knew how to handle all those changes, and one day he woke up and he didn't know me anymore. The Peter that he met was not the same Peter that was next to him a year later. My values, my way of seeing things, what I wanted—they were all different. Suddenly having a car or a nice apartment didn't matter to me. They would be nice to have, but it was more important to me to spend time doing volunteer work. Because we were not communicating, we couldn't keep up with the changes, and we became strangers. Eventually we broke up. Since then, I have done a lot of speaking and I have been on television and all that, so I'm very open about the fact that I am HIV-positive. Anyone who wants to become involved with me knows right up front that I have HIV, and it hasn't been a problem. It may be because the gay community in general has lived with this for so long and knows what HIV and AIDS is all about. I don't really worry about it because, for the first time in my life, I'm comfortable with who I am and I'm happy with myself. I don't feel like I need anybody else to make me feel good or make me feel like a whole person.

Is there anything you wish you knew when you were 14 or 15?

I wish that when I was 14 I had had the opportunity to speak to someone in an open and honest way about the things I was feeling emotionally and the things I was doing sexually. I think that, in my own way, I was crying out for help, and nobody saw it because I was an honor student, because I was a good kid, because I was quiet. I was not a rebel. I was not out doing drugs. I was not out getting into trouble. I just had this double life where I would go out at night and have fun, have sex, and nobody saw me.

When I was in tenth grade, a doctor came in to speak to us about AIDS. He came in a three-piece suit. He was very detached, and spoke down to us. He never even acknowledged that any of us could be experimenting with drugs or having sex. He acted like he was giving us this information just as our teachers had given us a problem to figure out the day before. He treated it like it was something we would probably never need to know but that he was required to talk about. This made me go back even deeper into my own little shell and not talk to anybody about it. And the only other people I got my information from were the same ones who were after me for sex, so they weren't giving me the right answers either.

Do you think it's harder for gay and lesbian teenagers?

Most teenagers, whether they are heterosexual or homosexual, won't talk to anyone they feel is judging them. In order for me to communicate with you, I have to feel comfortable around you. Because if I feel that you're judging me, I'm going to hide things.

For a gay teenager, it's even harder. We all need to show our sexuality in one way or another. We all need to validate our feelings. Heterosexual teenagers can show their sexuality in very simple ways that they take for granted. They do it by holding hands while they walk down the hall. They do it by writing letters to each other. They do it by writing "Mary loves Peter" on their folders. They don't have to have sex in order to be recognized as heterosexuals.

But gay teens can't write love letters to each other without the fear of being caught. They can't hold hands while they walk down the hall. They can't write "Peter loves David" on their folders. They can't be in a big group of kids and smile at each other or touch each other. They can't do any of the things that heterosexual teens can do to express their feelings. So the only way they can express themselves as lesbian or gay people is by having sex. Nothing else is allowed to them.

The whole idea of militancy, expressing ourselves in public and not caring what other people think, is relatively new, and it still hasn't extended to teenagers. Most teenagers, heterosexual or homosexual, haven't sorted out their identities. And the denial by the school systems and the government and society to address all of these issues makes it worse. The fact is that young people learn from their surroundings, and if the surroundings are giving the message that teenagers can't have sex and can't get AIDS, then the teenagers who are having sex are afraid to ask how they can get the disease.

What is the hardest part of AIDS education?

What I find to be a problem is that a lot of people want to tell the facts without explaining them. They say that HIV is transmitted through sex without explaining what sex is or why it can transmit HIV. And if you don't explain the why, then the fear remains. The fear only goes away with understanding. Once people understand the why, then they believe. I wish that for just one presentation all of America could sit inside me and see what is going on and see what kind of questions young people are asking me. Then they would have to realize that young people have very real questions.

The biggest mistake I as an AIDS educator see people making is that they don't give young people enough credit. They treat young people like they can't ever make good decisions. But if you give young people the facts, they will start to act responsibly. What it really comes down to is that many people are afraid to give young people the facts because they are afraid of losing control, of giving someone else the chance to make a choice and have a say in making decisions.

How can we overcome that?

The biggest problem we have with young people is that we aren't giving them options. With drugs, with sex, with everything, the only option we give them is to say no. But we never tell them how to say no, and most of the time we don't even tell them *why* to say no. We need to give them options. We need to talk about safer sex *and* abstinence. We have to give them the facts. Then they can pick up the facts and do what they want to with them. Some kids are going to choose to abstain, others aren't. Whenever you give someone choices, you run the risk that she or he isn't going to pick the choice that you want. But you have to give people that option.

Do you think about your future?

One of the things I have stopped doing is trying to have control that I don't have. Certain things I can control, certain things I can't. And I really don't have a lot of control over where I will be ten years from now. I can make plans, but it won't come out the way I plan it. When I think of my future, I think about starting college in the fall. That's my future right now.

Do you think about what might happen in terms of your disease?

I try not to, but that doesn't mean that I'm not dealing with it. Right now I'm very healthy. I take care of myself. The way I see it is that if death or sickness or a cure comes my way tomorrow, then I'll deal with it tomorrow. I don't have to deal with it now because it's not here.

Do you ever feel like something has been taken from you?

When I was in the hospital I dealt with a lot of anger and I had to figure out what it was that I was angry at. I discovered that I was angry at the government for not giving a damn about people with AIDS and being so indifferent. I was angry at society for being ignorant. And I was angry at the educational system for not educating me in an effective way about HIV and AIDS. Then I determined that the way to fight this was to do something about it. So when I got out of the hospital I joined ACT UP, I started speaking, and I started seeing changes.

Two years later, I found that I was still angry. Then I remembered something that happened when I was a child. My mother had a statue of Our Lady of Charity, the patron of Cuba, which had been passed down in her family for years. She loved it. One day she was dusting it, and she put it on a table. I came running into the house and hit the table. The statue flew across the room and broke into little pieces. My mother started screaming. I thought she was mad at me, so I ran away. About four hours later, I went back. My mother was waiting for me, and she gave me a kiss and a hug. She asked why I ran away, and I told her I thought she was angry at me. She explained to me that she was angry about what had happened, but not at me. She told me she was angry because she had lost something that was precious to her because she had not been responsible and cared for it properly, but that she was not angry at me for breaking it.

Remembering that helped me put my finger on what was bothering me. I was angry at the situation I was in, but not at any person or group, not even the person who gave me HIV. And I realized that I had the right to be angry because this thing that was precious to me, my life, was threatened because I didn't protect it enough.

I feel like I've been forced to deal with things that as a 19- or 20-year-old I shouldn't have to deal with. But that's been true all my life. I lived under a Communist government in Cuba and was extremely poor, and no kid should have to go through that. I came to a new country when I was eight. When I was 14, the most important person in my life, my mother, died. All my life I've been forced to deal with things that someone my age shouldn't have had to deal with. But at the same time, all the things that I gained from each situation did a lot to prepare me for dealing with HIV.

What do you think your life would be like if you hadn't tested positive?

I don't know. People always ask me if I would change anything I did, and I always feel like that's an "if" question. I promised myself that I would never think about or take seriously any "if" questions that I got, because two "ifs" just add up to another "if." The way I see it, if I could go back and change anything, maybe I could make myself rich or healthy or powerful. But I still might not like myself. And out of everything that's happened in my life, I've gained one thing, and that is that I like myself. I feel happy with who I am.

Sometimes when I look back over everything that's happened in the last 20 years, it's overwhelming to me. But then I look around at the people I've met, the friends who are living with AIDS, the people, like Sonia, who have died from it, and I see so much love and so much peace that it's incredible.

Sometimes it takes something as terrible as AIDS to make us realize what we really have. Even if AIDS goes away, it will have taught us all something. Years after the Holocaust, people are still fighting to make sure that no one forgets and that it never happens again. I think that AIDS will be the same way. AIDS is really the ultimate challenge because there is nothing, no other issue, that has touched so many peoples' lives and so many aspects of society. From the law to education, the AIDS crisis has challenged the way society views itself. Homelessness, poverty, crime—nothing cuts through lines of color, class, age, or sex like AIDS does. I think it will go down in history as the one thing that changed most the way we view our world.

Section Three:

KEEPING
safe

48.
Why is AIDS called a sexually transmitted disease?

A **sexually transmitted disease** (STD) is any infection or disease that is spread through sexual contact. Sexually transmitted diseases may also be called **venereal diseases**, or VD for short. Common sexually transmitted diseases include herpes, syphilis, and gonorrhea. Because one of the ways AIDS can be transmitted from one person to another is through sexual contact, it is considered a sexually transmitted disease, even though this is not the only way it can be spread.

49.
What is meant by the term *sexual contact?*

In this book, the term *sexual contact* refers to vaginal, anal, and oral sex. **Vaginal sex** is when a man's penis penetrates a woman's vagina. **Anal sex** is when a man's penis penetrates a man's or woman's **anus** or **rectum**. **Oral sex** is when a person's tongue or mouth comes into direct contact with a woman's vagina or a man's penis. Oral sex can also involve a person's tongue or mouth coming into contact with his or her partner's anus. This is called **rimming**.

Sexual contact can take place between a woman

and another woman, a man and a woman, or a man and another man. Sexual contact between a man and another man or a woman and another woman is called **homosexual sex**. Sexual contact between a woman and a man is called **heterosexual sex**.

50.

How is HIV spread through vaginal sex?

In vaginal sex, a man's penis comes into direct contact with a woman's vagina. The AIDS virus can pass from an infected man to a woman through the cells in the vaginal walls because the cells of a woman's vagina are filled with many blood vessels that can act as a direct route for the AIDS virus into the body. The virus could also enter through any cuts or ulcers that a woman may have in her vagina. It is important to remember that the AIDS virus is extremely small. A cut does not have to be very large to act as an entrance for HIV. A woman may not even be aware that she has any tiny cuts or tears in her vagina.

The virus can also pass from an infected woman to a man through abrasions or cuts on the penis or possibly through a man's **urethra**, the opening at the tip of the penis that urine and semen pass through. Again, these abrasions do not have to be large and may not even be noticeable.

Vaginal sex is the main means of infection in women 13–19 years old who have been diagnosed as having full-blown AIDS. It is estimated that 85% of women in this group contracted the AIDS virus in this way.

51.
How is HIV spread through anal sex?

In anal sex, a man's penis penetrates the anus of his partner and comes into direct contact with the rectum. As with vaginal sex, it is possible for the virus to enter the body directly through the cells of the rectal wall. Also, the walls of the rectum are very thin and can tear easily from the motion that occurs during anal sex, causing bleeding. If this happens, the virus has direct access to the bloodstream. HIV may also enter the penis of the penetrating partner during anal sex, either through breaks in the skin or through the urethra.

Many young men and women practice anal sex because it will prevent a woman from getting pregnant without having to worry about birth control or will allow her to say she is still a virgin because she has not had vaginal sex. They think that they cannot become infected through anal sex. This is extremely dangerous behavior, and it is accounting for a growing number of the cases of AIDS in young women. Anal sex is actually more likely to transmit the virus than vaginal sex.

52.
How is HIV spread through oral sex?

When oral sex is performed on a man, his penis comes into direct contact with his partner's mouth. If the man receiving oral sex has any cuts or abrasions on his penis, blood may be present. This blood can come into contact with any cuts, sores, or ulcers that the person performing oral sex has in his or her mouth, and HIV could enter the body through these breaks in the skin.

If the man ejaculates, or comes, in his partner's mouth, then there is direct contact with semen, which carries HIV. Again, the virus could infect the person performing oral sex through cuts in the mouth. Even if the man receiving oral sex removes his penis from his partner's mouth before ejaculating, there is the possibility that HIV can be found in pre-cum, the fluid produced before a man ejaculates.

There is also the possibility of infection when oral sex is performed on a woman. During oral sex with a woman, the partner's mouth comes into direct contact with vaginal fluids. HIV can be found in vaginal fluids, and if there are any cuts in the mouth of the person performing the oral sex, there is a chance of infection. If the woman receiving the oral sex is having her period, or **menstruating**, there is also blood present in the vagina. HIV is always found in the blood of infected people, so if an infected woman's menstrual blood comes into contact with an open cut in the mouth of the person performing oral sex, there is the risk of infection.

In rimming, oral sex in which a person's tongue and mouth come into contact with a partner's anus or rectum, there is the possibility of contracting HIV through small cuts in the rectal lining.

53.
Is the person receiving oral sex also at risk?

There is a small risk for the person receiving oral sex. If a woman's partner is infected and has any cuts or ulcers in the mouth, HIV-infected blood from her partner may come into direct contact with the cells of her vagina. These cells may act as a direct route for HIV into the bloodstream.

For a man receiving oral sex, there is the possibility that infected blood from his partner's mouth may come into contact with his urethra or with cuts on his penis, which may be a way for HIV to enter the body.

54.
Is oral sex really that risky?

Although oral sex is much less risky than anal or vaginal sex, unprotected oral sex does put you in direct contact with bodily fluids that can transmit the AIDS virus, and it therefore puts you at risk for getting AIDS. Oral sex can also spread other STDs such as herpes, syphilis, and gonorrhea.

55.
Is all sex dangerous?

Any activity where there is the possibility of a person's bodily fluids coming into contact with another person's bloodstream is unsafe, so the only real form of completely safe sex is **abstinence**, or not having sex at all. This does not mean that you have to live in fear of having sex or that you can never have sex. What it means is that you must know the facts about how HIV is transmitted and how to protect yourself. There are many sexual activities that minimize the risk of HIV infection. These activities are referred to as **safer sex** because, while they do not completely eliminate the possibility of infection, they make sex safer for both people involved.

56.
What are some safer sex practices?

Safer sex practices are anything you can think of to do that does not involve your bloodstream coming into direct contact with your partner's bodily fluids. Safer sex can include having anal or vaginal sex using a **condom** (rubber) or oral sex using a condom or **dental dam**. Safer sex can also include kissing, touching, massage, and **masturbation**. Masturbation with another person should be avoided, however, if either partner has sores on the hands or sexual organs to avoid coming into contact with infected vaginal fluids or semen.

57.
What is a condom?

A condom, commonly called a rubber, is a sheath made of latex rubber that fits over the penis and prevents a man's pre-cum and semen from entering his partner during oral, anal, or vaginal sex. When a man comes, the semen is trapped inside the condom and cannot reach his partner. Condoms are sold in most drugstores, and you do not need a prescription or have to be a certain age to buy them. Condoms were once mainly used to prevent pregnancy, but now they are very important in preventing the spread of sexually transmitted diseases, including AIDS.

58.
How do you use a condom?

For the most protection, condoms should be used whenever a man's penis is going to come into contact with his partner's mouth, vagina, or anus. For a diagram of how to use a condom, see the illustration on the next page.

A condom should be put on the erect, or hard, penis *before* any penetration happens. Do not try to put the condom on a limp penis. The condom package should be opened carefully, so that the condom does not rip. Never open a condom package with your teeth; it can put a hole in the rubber.

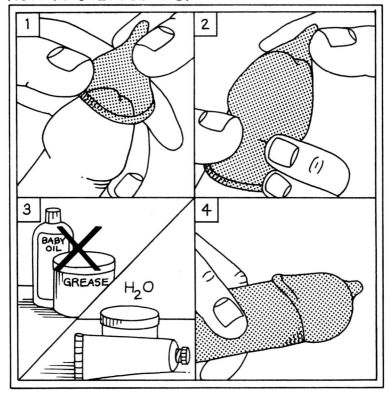

Step 1: Place the condom over the tip of the penis. Make sure that you leave room at the tip for the semen to collect after ejaculation. If you don't, the condom may burst when you ejaculate. Many condoms have a special end, called a reservoir tip, that is designed to collect the semen.

Step 2: Holding the tip in place, roll the condom gently down the full length of the penis. If you have a **foreskin**, pull it back before putting on a rubber. Do not unroll the condom before putting it on the penis. If you try to put an unrolled condom onto an erect penis, it could rip. Gently pinch the tip of the condom to squeeze out any air that is present and run your fingers down the sides to push out any air that might be trapped inside. Air pockets can cause the rubber to break during sexual activity.

Step 3: During anal and vaginal sex, it is important to use some kind of **lubricant**. This helps prevent the rubber from breaking. It is also a good idea to put a dab of lubricant on the head of the penis before putting on a condom, since this is the area that will encounter the most pressure during sexual activity. Always use a lubricant that contains mostly water, like K-Y, Corn Huskers Lotion, or one of the many lubricants sold especially for use in sexual activity. Do not use baby oil, Crisco, Vaseline, or mineral oil. These contain mostly oil and can cause a condom to break.

Step 4: After a man ejaculates, or comes, he should hold the base of the condom firmly and remove his penis from his partner's anus, mouth, or vagina *before* his penis becomes limp. This prevents any semen from leaking out of the condom as the penis shrinks in size. Always dispose of a condom after you have used it. Never use it again. Also, do not use a condom with an expiration date that has passed or that has been in your wallet or glove compartment for a long time. It will be brittle and can break more easily. The expiration date for a condom should be printed on the wrapper or on the box it came in. Before engaging in any further sexual activity, it is a good idea for a man to wash his penis. This removes any semen that may be on the skin.

If you have never used condoms, buy a package and practice putting them on. If you want to, you can practice on a banana or a carrot.

59.
Do all types of condoms offer protection against the transmission of HIV?

No. You should only use latex (rubber) condoms. There is another kind made from animal membranes (often called skins), but these are not effective in preventing the transmission of diseases. They are made out of a material that has pores in it, and these pores can allow HIV or any other virus to pass through and come into contact with the body. Also avoid the condoms that fit only over the head of the penis (called tip condoms) and do not extend the full length of the penis. These condoms can leak very easily and offer no protection against pregnancy, the AIDS virus, or any other sexually transmitted disease.

It is a good idea to use condoms that come with **nonoxynol-9**, a chemical that kills sperm and may help prevent the transmission of the AIDS virus. Today, many condoms are coated with nonoxynol-9. If the ones you use aren't, you should buy a lubricant that has nonoxynol-9 in it. Condoms and lubricants that contain nonoxynol-9 will be so labeled on the package.

60.
Are condoms 100% effective?

If used properly, condoms offer the best protection against the AIDS virus and other sexually transmitted diseases. But it is possible for a condom to break. While condoms are tested for strength before they are sold, they do sometimes break as a result of the motion that occurs during sex. If you are worried about this happening, you can wear two condoms, one over the other.

61.
What do I do if a condom breaks?

If a condom breaks during sex, you can usually feel it. If you feel a condom break, stop the sexual activity immediately. The man should hold the base of the condom firmly and pull out as soon as possible. Before resuming sexual activity, it is important that the man wash his penis and put on another condom.

62.
How can I protect myself during oral sex?

It is recommended that men receiving oral sex wear a condom, just as they would during vaginal or anal sex. This protects both the person performing oral sex and the man receiving it.

For protection while performing oral sex with a woman, there is a product called a dental dam. A dental dam is a sheet of latex rubber, the same rubber used in condoms. It is placed over a woman's vagina and held in place with the fingers. This dam prevents a person's mouth from coming into direct contact with a woman's vaginal fluids. Dental dams are often sold in drugstores. If you do not have dental dams, it is also possible to use a plastic wrap such as Saran Wrap. However, do not use the microwavable kind. It has tiny holes in the surface that can allow the virus to pass through. It is also possible to make a dental dam by cutting a condom down one side and spreading it open to make a sheet. A dental dam should also be used when performing rimming, in which case the dam is stretched over the anus of the person who is receiving the sex.

63.
I'm too embarrassed to buy condoms. What can I do?

Buying condoms should not make you feel embarrassed. They are easily available at most drugstores, and if you don't see them, you can always ask. If you feel embarrassed, you can always buy something ordinary like gum or toothpaste along with the condoms. Some schools are now distributing condoms to students. You can also frequently get free condoms at local health agencies such as Planned Parenthood or an AIDS information center.

Remember, if you are ready to have sex, you should be ready to buy condoms. Also, it was once believed that it was a man's responsibility to buy and wear condoms. Today it is everyone's responsibility. Many manufacturers are now selling condoms aimed at female purchasers. Women who are having sex should not be embarrassed or ashamed to buy condoms and ask their partners to wear them. No one has ever died of embarrassment, but they have died because they were too embarrassed to buy and use condoms.

64.
What can I do if my religion prohibits the use of condoms?

People whose religions prohibit the use of condoms have to make a personal choice. The fact is that if you are having unprotected sex, you are putting yourself at risk for contracting the AIDS virus. AIDS is not a disease that only "bad" people get, and it is not a punishment for having sex. It is a sexually transmitted disease, and it can kill you.

65.
My partner says that if I love him I won't make him wear condoms. What should I do?

Using condoms is not about trust or proving your love for someone; it is about protecting yourself from a deadly virus. You must remember that when you have sexual intercourse with someone, you are also being exposed to the diseases of every single person that your partner has ever had sex with. Unless you know absolutely everything about your partner, you don't know where she or he has been before meeting you. Even if she or he appears completely healthy, the AIDS virus could still be in his or her blood. Your partner might not even know she or he is infected.

If your partner says that you won't make him wear a condom if you love him, he is really saying that he doesn't care enough about you or himself to protect you both from AIDS. And if you don't ask him to wear a condom, then you are saying that you don't care enough about yourself to protect your life. Many women who have been infected say that they did not use condoms because they wanted their boyfriends to know that they loved them and thought that their boyfriends would leave them if they made them wear condoms. Now these women are fighting a deadly virus and stand to lose more than just the men they were trying to "prove" themselves to.

66.
How can I talk to my partner about safer sex?

Talking about sex can be difficult, but it is much more difficult to live with the consequences of not talking about it. The best way to bring up the subject of safer sex with someone you have been with for some time is to simply start talking about AIDS and how you feel about it. This will naturally bring up the subject of safer sex. You might want to give your partner a brochure or a book such as this one. Or you can say something like, "Did you know that a lot of teenagers are getting AIDS? What do you think about that?" This should start a discussion that will get around to safer sex. If your partner is a man, you might want to buy some of the fancy condoms available and give them to him as a gift. He'll get the message.

If you have just met someone and are thinking about participating in sexual activity, it is very important that you let that person know right up front that you practice safer sex. You can do this by saying something like, "I am really attracted to you, and I would like to have sex. But I want you to know that I always practice safer sex." If the person reacts negatively, then chances are that she or he isn't worth the trouble. You must do this *before* you begin to engage in sexual activity. Once you start, it is hard to stop and talk about what you are going to do next!

67.
How do I say no to risky behavior?

Saying no to risky behavior can be very hard, but the consequences of not saying no are even harder to live with. A few minutes of pleasure may seem worth the risk at the time, but is it worth trading a long, healthy life for? Remember that you are an important person, and taking care of yourself should be the most important thing in your life. Participating in risky behavior is treating yourself badly, and anyone who says he or she loves you but tries to get you to do something that is not in your best interests is lying to you. Sometimes we all feel depressed or down, and it seems like nothing we do matters. When we feel like this, it is easier to justify participating in risky activities. But try to think ahead to the future. Do you want to be living a healthy, active life, or do you want to be fighting off a deadly disease?

If someone is pressuring you to participate in behavior that is risky, leave the situation. If you are at a party where people are shooting drugs, leave. If you are being pressured by a boyfriend or girlfriend to have risky sex, then you must let that person know exactly how you feel. Tell him or her that you want to protect both of you from any diseases. Let your friend know that loving someone means caring about what happens to her or him; it does not mean putting someone you care about at risk for contracting HIV.

68.
How do drugs and alcohol affect risky behavior?

Drugs and alcohol affect your ability to think clearly. When you have been drinking or using drugs, you are not in full control of a situation, and you might do things that you wouldn't do otherwise, like have sex without using condoms or share needles to inject drugs. Drugs and alcohol also decrease the body's ability to fight off infection, making it easier for the AIDS virus to invade the immune system.

69.

My friends say that "real" men don't wear condoms. I don't want to look dumb, so what can I do?

Peer pressure can be a very powerful thing. It is hard to do something you know is right when all of your friends are telling you it's wrong. In some cultures, it is believed that men who wear condoms are weak or afraid. It is also sometimes believed that women who insist that the men they have sex with wear condoms have something to hide or don't trust the men enough. These are all deadly ways of thinking. Being a real man means taking responsibility for your life and the life of the person you are having sex with. Being a real woman means caring enough about yourself to stay healthy. If someone says that "real" men and women don't practice safer sex, they are only showing their ignorance.

70.

Can spermicides kill the AIDS virus?

Spermicides, substances used to prevent pregnancy, are designed to kill sperm. A spermicide can be a jelly or foam that is inserted into a woman's vagina, or it can come in the form of a pill that is inserted into the vagina before sex. Some condoms also come coated with spermicides. While spermicides kill the sperm that cause pregnancy, they are not designed to prevent sexually transmitted diseases. Using a spermicide may help slow down the AIDS virus, but it will not necessarily kill it. And a spermicide alone does nothing to prevent HIV from coming into contact with your bloodstream. A spermicide can be used *along with* a condom to add extra protection, but it should never be used *instead* of a condom.

71.
Is being on the pill or using a diaphragm enough to protect me from the AIDS virus?

Birth control pills are designed to prevent pregnancy by affecting the hormones that control the reproductive cycle. They are not designed to prevent any sexually transmitted diseases, including AIDS. The pill cannot prevent infected blood or semen from coming into contact with your vagina and has no effect on killing the AIDS virus.

A **diaphragm** is a rubber barrier that is inserted into a woman's vagina before sex. It is designed to prevent sperm from entering a woman's **cervix** and impregnating her. A diaphragm will not prevent the spread of AIDS or most other sexually transmitted diseases, because it still allows contact between the woman's vaginal walls and her partner's semen. **Contraceptive sponges**, sponges that are inserted into a woman's vagina before sex to absorb semen, also do nothing to prevent sexually transmitted diseases. The *only* effective means of helping to prevent the transmission of HIV during sexual activity is wearing a condom.

72.
Will douching after sex kill the AIDS virus?

HIV enters the walls of the rectum or vagina very soon after contact, so **douching** after sex has no effect on preventing transmission of the AIDS virus. In fact, douching may actually do more harm by washing infected semen or blood further up into or around the vagina or rectum and giving HIV another chance of coming into contact with vaginal or rectal surfaces.

73.
Is pulling out before ejaculation safe?

Pulling out, or removing the penis from a partner's mouth, rectum, or vagina before ejaculating, reduces the risk of infection, but it is still not completely effective. The AIDS virus may be present in pre-cum, the fluid that is excreted by the penis before a man ejaculates, and can be transmitted that way. Pulling out also has no effect on protecting the man who is performing anal or vaginal sex, since his unprotected penis will still be exposed to his partner's bodily fluids.

74.
Is deep, or French, kissing okay?

Although the AIDS virus is found in small amounts in saliva, deep, or French, kissing does not present much of a danger. You would have to swallow about a gallon of your partner's saliva in order to get enough HIV to be dangerous. Still, to be completely safe, it is recommended that people with cuts or sores in their mouths or on their tongues do not participate in kissing where large amounts of saliva are exchanged.

75.
I've been with the same partner for two years. Do we have to worry?

If both you and your partner have tested negative for the AIDS virus, and if you both are completely **monogamous**, meaning that you have sex only with each other, and do not participate in any other risky behavior, then you are probably safe. Remember that it is possible for HIV to be present in a person's body for several years before any symptoms appear. Unless you know everything your partner has ever done and everything that every person your partner has had sex or shared needles with has done, you cannot be certain that she or he does not have HIV infection unless that person is tested.

76.

How is HIV spread by using needles?

Using needles to inject drugs means that a needle is inserted into the body. This needle comes into contact with your blood. When you pull the needle out, some of this blood is drawn back up into the hollow core of the needle and also into the **syringe**, the hollow plastic tube that is attached to the needle and holds the drug being injected. If someone else uses the needle without cleaning it, the blood from the first user comes into contact with the blood of the second user. Sharing dirty needles is the same as injecting the AIDS virus directly into your bloodstream.

When we talk about getting AIDS from needles, people usually think only about people who shoot up, or use needles to inject drugs like heroin or cocaine. But the AIDS virus can also be transmitted by sharing needles to inject steroids, drugs used by bodybuilders and athletes to increase their muscle mass.

77.

I use intravenous drugs. How can I keep safe?

If you are going to use intravenous drugs and share needles, you are going to continue to put yourself at risk for HIV infection. If you feel you must shoot drugs, you must never share needles with anyone. If you do share needles, you must clean them with bleach as illustrated in the diagram below.

Step 1: Fill the syringe to the top with common household bleach (like Clorox), then empty it into a sink or toilet. Fill it up and empty it again.

HOW TO CLEAN A SYRINGE

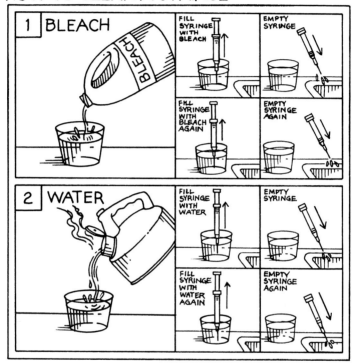

Step 2: Fill the needle with water that has been boiled and empty it. Fill it again with water and empty it. If you cannot boil the water, you can use hot water out of the faucet.

This is the *only* way to effectively clean a needle. Boiling a needle in water alone will not clean it enough, nor will holding the needle over a burning match or candle.

Kaye

On February 22, 1992, Kaye Brown, a high-school senior with
a lifelong dream of a career in the military, tried to enlist in
the United States army. She was told she was a pound and a
half over the weight requirement for military service and was

given a week to lose the extra weight. At that time, she also
gave blood so that the necessary tests required for acceptance
into the army could be done.

A few days later, Kaye received a letter asking her to
report back to the military entrance processing station to
discuss the results of her medical examination. On March 2,
1992, she went back, and was told that she had tested
positive for the AIDS virus.

In the short time that Kaye has known her HIV status,
she has devoted much of her time to working for AIDS
Foundation Houston as a peer educator. She also attends
high school full time and plans to enter college in the fall to
study accounting.

Did you have any idea that you were infected with HIV?

No, it came as a complete shock.

How did they tell you?

I got a certified letter saying that I had a "potentially serious condition of a personal nature." That's exactly how they put it. They asked me to come down to the station with my recruiter. So I went down, and they told me in front of a doctor, a nurse, and the commanding officer that I had tested HIV-positive.

What did you think the condition in the letter was?

I really did not know. It crossed my mind briefly that it might be AIDS. I think it would have crossed the mind of any sexually active person. But I didn't think that's what they were going to say. I didn't suspect anyone I had been with. But I did know that, whatever it was, it was going to ruin my career.

Did they offer any support after telling you that you were positive?

They gave me a list of specialists that they told me I could go to. And they gave me some information that explained what HIV and AIDS are. Then they asked me if I wanted to retest to make sure that the results were correct, because they had tested about sixty other girls at the same time, and maybe my results had gotten mixed up with someone else's. So I retested, and it came back confirming the positive results. But after that, they said their hands were tied. They can't offer you treatment and help. But they do tell you that you need to get help.

It sounds like the army will provide medical advice but nothing emotional.

No, nothing like that. The only emotional support I got from them right then was when someone asked me if I was all right. Because I had this look of complete shock on my face for a while. I couldn't speak, but I shook my head to let them know that I was still responding to the world. The guys that told me that I was positive didn't give me much support. But later on, they did help me get into some medical programs when I had trouble getting in.

My recruiter was my lifesaver. He gave me personal counseling to help me get over the initial shock. He keeps in contact with me to make sure that I'm okay and asks if I need anything.

Did you feel like the army was judging you?

No, I didn't. I really believe that they helped me as much as they possibly could.

What was your first reaction after the initial shock wore off?

They told me that, because I was HIV-positive, I wasn't eligible to serve in any of the armed forces. And that was what I was mainly concentrating on at first, not getting into the military. Because I had been trying for so long to get in. And I was really upset about *that*. The fact that I was now HIV-positive didn't hit me until later. That really hurt, the fact that I had worked so hard and now couldn't be in the army.

You really weren't think about being positive?

Not at first. After I got over the fact that I couldn't be in the army, then I had to deal with the fact that I'm HIV-positive and I felt embarrassed by it more than scared. I was afraid of how I was going to tell my family. I didn't think I could possibly tell them.

Have you told them?

Yes, I told them the same day because I wanted to get it over with. I knew they were going to have to find out anyway.

How did they respond?

My mom, I guess she thought someone was trying to take me away from her. Her first reaction was to grab me and hold me, to try to protect me. My sister gave me this I-told-you-so speech because she was always telling me to slow down. And my cousin was, like, "I'm not glad that you have it, but I'm glad that it's not me." They all had different reactions, but in the end everybody supported me. Nobody cut me off.

How about your friends?

You know how friends can be. They smile at your face and then talk behind your back. But I'm getting a lot of support. And that's all I need, someone to say to me, "I support you." But there's still rumors out there, stories out there, that I did this and that or I'm like this or that. And I know there have to be some people who say they support me and then talk about me.

Do you get mad at them?

I get mad at their ignorance. I get mad when I walk down the hallway at school and hear, "That's the one. She has AIDS." And I want to turn around and shout, "I don't have AIDS; I have HIV." But I don't do that because they have an opportunity to learn, and if they don't bother, then I'm not going to waste my breath on them.

So the kids at school don't give you any trouble?

No. And I think that's because most of them are being educated about HIV and AIDS. They know you can't come by it through casual contact, so they know they can't get it by sitting near me or using the same bathroom or if I breathe on them or anything.

Have you determined how you were infected?

I know it was through sexual intercourse, because I've never done any of the other things that can transmit HIV. And I think it was in November of 1991 because a lot of people, when they are first infected, get flulike symptoms or rashes, both of which I had shortly after Thanksgiving.

Do you know who you contracted it from?

No, because a lot of the people I was with don't want to go get tested. A lot of people don't want to know if they have it. And some people have said to me, well, maybe whoever gave it to you knew that he was infected. I have a hard time with that, because I can't believe anyone would do something like that. But I know it does happen. I think that the person had it and didn't know it. Then after I got tested, he went and found out he was positive and was too embarrassed to tell me.

How do the men that you have to go back and tell react?

At first they don't believe it. Then they ask how I got infected. Then they want to know if my testing positive means that they have it, and I have to explain it all to them and tell them that they have to get tested. Most of them are scared, and I tell them that I'll go with them to get tested, I'll hold their hand and support them, but that getting tested is up to them. And I tell them that if they have any questions, they can come to me, but most of them don't. I do everything I can.

Have any of them gotten angry?
Just one. He was very angry at first, but then he realized that he couldn't be angry at me because I didn't know I was positive when I was with him. Then he said, "How can you have it, you look so clean. I didn't know you were dirty." And I said, "I'm not dirty. This does not make me dirty." I think he just had to get that anger out, and once he did, he asked a lot of questions.

I think a lot of people react with anger at first.
I know that was my first reaction. Before I tested positive and was still scared of AIDS, I remember I told someone that if anyone should have AIDS, it should be me, and if I ever found out I had it no one would ever, ever see me again because I was just going to close up in my house, lock the doors, pull the shades, and never come out again because I was so scared. But that's not what's happened. Now, my whole attitude's changed.

Why do you think that's happened?
For me, it's because now I feel responsible. I feel I have the responsibilty to let other people know that this can happen to anyone. At school, I'm on the honor roll, French team, accounting team, debate team, speech club, drama, all those things. I do all these things at

school, and I'm not a delinquent or anything, I don't get into trouble. And still this happened to me.

A lot of kids hear about what happened to Magic Johnson, and they know HIV and AIDS are out there, but they think that it will never happen to them. They think that it only happens to people with a lot of money who can afford to buy and do things that they can't, like having money makes you able to do the things that transmit HIV. I'm here to say that it can happen to them, for the simple reason that it can happen to anyone. The point I'm trying to get across to kids is that it doesn't have to happen; it is a preventable condition. It can happen to everyday normal high-school kids. High-school, junior-high, even elementary-school kids, as long as they put themselves at risk.

You knew about AIDS before you were tested.

Yeah, I did. I had had a couple of brief AIDS-education classes, and I knew that you got it from having unprotected sex and shooting drugs.

But you still weren't using condoms?

I had the attitude that, if the guy wanted to use a condom, fine. If he didn't, then I wasn't going to push the issue.

Do you think a lot of girls have that attitude?

Oh, yes. They don't demand it or make the guys wear condoms because they don't want to go through the hassle. A lot of guys don't want to wear one, and they refuse to. And most girls don't want to go through the fight of making them use one. A lot of girls get scared that, if they ask a man to use a condom, he's going to think she's dirty or unsafe, and then rumors will start about her. So there's a lot of fear on the girl's part that guys will think she's unclean and her reputation will be ruined. And the guys don't think they can get AIDS in the first place.

Don't they worry about pregnancy?
Guys tell the girls to take the pill so they don't have to worry about it. Or girls will have anal sex because they don't have to worry about getting pregnant and they can still say that they're virgins. That can be a deadly mistake. A lot of people think that getting pregnant is the biggest thing you have to worry about, but that's not true. There are a lot of other things out there.

Before you tested positive, what was your picture of someone who had AIDS?
Somebody who was really thin and sick. Because I thought HIV and AIDS were the same thing. I thought that someone with HIV automatically got AIDS and died. But that's not true.

So when you tested, suddenly you're the only one you know who has HIV?
Exactly. I knew it was out there, and I knew that a lot of people were infected. But suddenly it seemed like I was the only one. Nobody else I knew was coming up to me

and saying, "Hey, I have it, too. I'm scared, too. Let's talk."

You were only diagnosed about a month ago. How did you educate yourself so quickly?

After I found out, I went to talk with our school's support counselor. She put me in contact with AIDS Foundation Houston. I sat in on some of their presentations and educated myself that way. Then they offered me a job as a peer educator, and I went through training. Now I go to schools, juvenile detention centers, runaway teen homes, anywhere I can talk.

What do you find that people's biggest misconception about AIDS is?

That having HIV and AIDS are the same thing. They think that everyone with HIV is sick.

What do people ask you the most?

How I got it. They also want to know if I know who gave it to me, how my parents reacted, if I'm angry at the guy who gave it to me. A lot of people also comment that I'm brave, but I don't agree with that.

Why don't you think you're brave?

Because my conception of someone who's brave is someone who risks their life to save someone else. They know what they're up against, and they do it anyway. But I didn't volunteer to get HIV. If someone had offered me HIV on a platter, I would have said no. But because it happened to me, I'm handling it the best way I can. I'm not doing anything to be heroic. I feel responsible, but I don't feel brave. I feel responsible for other people, as well as for myself.

Is that what keeps you going?
That's what keeps me going. Plus, I used to be a mother. My son died when he was a few months old, and I feel responsible to the kids that are growing up now, because a lot of these kids will lose their parents to AIDS.

Why do you think so many kids refuse to think about HIV and AIDS?
There are a lot of kids out there who don't want to think about the things that can transmit HIV because they're afraid that people will think they're bad kids if they admit that they're doing those things. It's easier to point the finger at other people. The most satisfaction I've had since testing positive was when a classmate told me that a lot of the seniors got together after they heard I tested positive and none of them pointed a finger or said I was bad or anything. What they did do was talk about AIDS, and a lot of them decided to get tested. That made me feel good.

Did you have a boyfriend when you tested positive?
Yes, I did. He and I are no longer together because he needed some time to cope with it all. And I said, "Well, time is not something that I have a lot of. If you want time to cope, fine, but I'm not waiting around." So we aren't together because I feel that, if he can't be with me

now during this, he wouldn't be there for me later. I'm not angry, because I know he's scared, but it makes me mad that he gave in so easily and worried more about what he would tell his family than about me. When I first got the letter, when he knew something was wrong but not what it was, he was the pillar of strength. Then, the day I went for the results, he didn't want to know.

Has he been tested?
It took a lot of effort, but I got him to go. But the last I heard, he never went for his results, so I don't know if he's infected or not.

Is thinking about another relationship hard?
The hardest thing for me right now is knowing that I have to find someone who accepts me first as a person and then accepts the fact that this person has HIV. He has to accept both, because one won't work without the other. A lot of people see only the HIV and forget that you are a person with thoughts and feelings. Or they see the person and don't want to see the HIV. I have found someone who accepts both parts of me, but it's hard for him because he doesn't want to see me suffer and go through pain.

How do you feel about that?
I understand it, because I wouldn't want to see anyone I cared about go through pain. And it makes me feel responsible for myself and for him. I want to keep myself healthy, so that I can be around for as long as possible.

Do you ever think about the possibility of there being a cure?

I think I've accepted the fact that there may *not* be one. I know that there is the possibility of a vaccine and new treatments. But as far as a cure, I don't put my head in the clouds.

Do you ever feel like someone's taken something from you?

When I think about the military. But then I kick myself in the butt because I did this to myself. Nobody did it to me, and it could have been prevented. I wanted to be in the army so badly, and I think about how hard I trained to get there. And I think about not having a child or maybe not having a husband. Because I always said I wasn't getting married until I was 32. I wanted time to shop around. Now, I don't even know if I'll be here when I'm 32.

You don't sound angry or bitter about anything.

Angry? No, no. There's really no one to be angry at except myself, and that's not going to get me anywhere. Talking to kids helps, because it makes it feel worthwhile. I mean, I'm not glad I have this, but I can do something useful with it, and that makes me feel good. And my family helps. They don't treat me any differently. They still drink out of the same glass and all that, and that helps. That makes me feel normal.

Are there days when you don't feel normal?

The only time I don't feel normal is when it comes to personal relationships. When I'm with a guy one-on-one, I feel like it's an issue then.

I don't think someone who hasn't been infected or affected by HIV or AIDS could ever possibly know exactly what someone with HIV or AIDS goes through. For instance, cancer is, usually, a terminal disease. But there's a totally different reaction when you tell someone you have HIV than there is when you tell them you have cancer, because people automatically assume that people with HIV or AIDS are dirty. But cancer seems natural, and it shouldn't have happened. People feel sorry for people with cancer, but they blame people with AIDS because it's associated with sex and drugs.

Do you ever forget you are HIV-positive?

Every morning. It's not until something reminds me that I remember. I'll forget, and then someone will say something to bring me back, and I'll think, "Oh, yeah, I'm infected."

People say that, because I have HIV, I can't do this or I can't do that. But I'm an independent-minded person. I feel more comfortable when I'm the host in my own home than when I'm a guest in someone else's home. And my body is my home. I feel comfortable with the idea that I am the host to HIV. I am not the guest of HIV. So, in that sense, I run HIV; HIV does not run me. There may come a day when I have to give in to it, but I'm not going out without a fight.

Do you worry about what could happen?

I know that somewhere down the line I probably will get sick. And every now and then I do feel different, like everyone else is freezing and I'll feel like I have a fever. Then I think that maybe it's the HIV. But I can't start blaming HIV every time I feel a little bit sick. I don't want it to become an excuse.

Where do you think you'll be in the next five or ten years?

In five years, I will have my master's degree in accounting and I'll be working toward becoming a CPA. That's as far as I've gotten so far.

Do you think people see women with HIV infection differently than they see men with it?

Yes. Because AIDS is considered a sexually transmitted disease, a lot of people see women with AIDS as dirty. They think only prostitutes or women who sleep around a lot get AIDS. If a woman has HIV, then she's a slut. But if a man has it, it's because he's such a ladies' man, and they feel sorry for him.

What one thing should young people know about HIV and AIDS?

That it happens, and it happens to us. And it doesn't have to. If you're grown-up enough to do whatever you're doing, be grown-up enough to have your bases covered. Because it's happening to us more and more, and if we don't slow down and start taking care of ourselves, our whole generation is going to be wiped out.

Do you have any regrets?

I wish I knew a year ago where I would be now. Because if I did, then I would have done things differently. I wouldn't have stopped having sex, but I would have used condoms. But no regrets. I've asked myself a lot of times why I got involved with that jerk, whoever he was. But I don't regret anything because each experience taught me something, and I'm a sucker for knowledge.

And I'm going to learn from HIV, too. I'm learning every day from it. I'm learning about medical things that I never would have known about. I'm learning about people's attitudes, and I'm learning about myself.

Testing

&

Beyond

78.
How can I find out if I am infected with HIV?

The only way to find out if you are infected with the AIDS virus is to have a blood test designed to test for the presence of HIV antibodies or the AIDS virus itself. While these tests are frequently referred to as AIDS tests, this is inaccurate. There is no test for AIDS, only tests for the virus that can lead to AIDS.

79.
Who should be tested for HIV?

Anyone who has participated in risky behavior within the last fifteen years should be tested for HIV. This includes anyone who has had sexual intercourse without a condom, used IV drugs, injected steroids, or had a transfusion or transplant. You do not have to be a certain age to be tested for HIV, and you do not need anyone's permission.

Deciding to take the test for the AIDS virus is not a game. You should think very carefully before making the decision. Many people get tested without thinking about what their test results will mean. They just want to reassure themselves that they are fine. Then they are completely unprepared when they test positive.

Plan ahead and think seriously about how you

will react to your test result. If you do test positive, do you know of support groups that can help you deal with your feelings and give you reliable information about what to do next? Will your family and friends be supportive of your test? How will a positive test result change your life?

If your result is negative, are you still going to be responsible about participating in safer sex or needle cleaning? Some people see a negative test result as a license to practice risky behavior. They think that they are somehow immune to the AIDS virus because they have not yet contracted it.

After thinking these things through, you may decide that you are not ready to take an HIV test yet. This is okay. It is better to wait until you feel prepared to deal with your test result than to get tested too early and be unprepared for what could happen. Remember, however, that the earlier the AIDS virus is detected, the earlier treatment for HIV infection can begin. The longer a person waits, the more time HIV has to damage her or his immune system.

80.
What will an HIV test tell me?

An HIV test will tell you if your body has been infected with HIV, the virus that causes AIDS. Depending on what kind of test you have, it may also tell you how long the virus has been in your body and to what extent it has spread through your body.

81.

How soon after a person is infected with HIV will the virus show up in a test?

The test for the AIDS virus is actually a test for the presence of antibodies to HIV that the body produces once it realizes it has been infected. The body will usually produce enough antibodies to be detected within six weeks of becoming infected. This length of time between becoming infected and when the body has produced enough antibodies to be detected by a test is called the **window period**.

82.

Where can I get an HIV antibody test?

Most cities have free testing sites where you can go for an HIV antibody test. Look in the phone book or call one of the numbers at the back of this book. You can also have the test done through your doctor or through an organization like Planned Parenthood or a pregnancy counseling center. There are some places that try to take advantage of people who are scared about HIV infection by promising them quick results for a fee, but these places are unreliable. You should never go to a place that advertises HIV testing and results in one or two hours or charges a lot of money. For reliable results and solid information, you should go only to a doctor or a clinic that specializes in AIDS testing.

83.

What is the difference between the different places offering HIV tests?

The main difference between places that offer HIV testing has to do with who knows the results of your test. It is recommended that you go to a center that offers **anonymous** testing. This means that no one at the clinic will know your name or who you are. When you go for the test, you will be assigned a number. No one will take your name. When you either call or come back for your results, you will give them your identification number. This way, your name is never associated with your test results.

If you go to a private doctor or a clinic that does not have anonymous testing, your results will not be completely anonymous, they will be **confidential**. This means that your doctor or the clinic will know your name and your test results, as will the lab where the test is done. Doctors and labs are never supposed to release the results of tests, but mistakes do sometimes happen. To be absolutely sure that you and only you will know your test results, it is recommended that you go to an anonymous test site.

Recently, some states have considered passing laws that would do away with anonymous testing. Before you get tested, find out if the testing center you have chosen offers completely anonymous or only confidential testing.

84.
What Are the different types of tests for HIV?

There are three kinds of tests that are used to check for HIV. The most commonly used type of test is an **antibody test**. This test checks the blood for the presence of antibodies to the AIDS virus, the proteins that your immune system manufactures when it senses that it has been invaded by HIV. The antibody test that is used in most HIV tests is called the **ELISA** test. ELISA stands for *enzyme-linked immunosorbent assay*. A second type of antibody test is called the **Western blot** test. It, too, tests for the presence of HIV-related proteins, but it is more specific than the ELISA test. It is also more difficult and expensive to perform, so it is usually only used to double-check positive or inconclusive ELISA results.

The second type of HIV test is called an **antigen test**. This type of test is used to double-check a positive result to an antibody test. It actually checks for the presence of HIV itself, not just antibodies to the virus. Specific kinds of antigen tests are used to search for specific parts of the AIDS virus, and are often used along with antibody tests to tell what stage of HIV infection a person is in.

The third kind of test, a **viral culture,** is a test in which laboratory workers actually try to grow HIV from a sample of a person's cells or bodily fluids. This test is always done in conjunction with the other two types of tests because, even when a person is definitely infected, it is not always possible to get the AIDS virus to reproduce outside the body.

85.
What will happen when I go for an HIV test?

When you call about taking an HIV test, the person you talk to will make an appointment for you. Depending on where you live, this may be the same day but could be two or three weeks from the day you call. If you are going to a place that offers anonymous testing, you will be given an identification number. When you go for your test, you will give the testers your identification number. This number will be used to identify you without anyone having to know your name.

Before the actual test, you will most likely talk to a counselor specializing in AIDS. The counselor may ask you some questions about your past sexual activity, whether you have ever had a transfusion, or whether you have ever used drugs. She or he may also ask you if you think your test will be positive or how you will react if your test is positive. Counselors do this so that they can identify people who may need additional counseling or whose tests are more likely than those of others to be positive for HIV. The counselor will then give you the opportunity to ask any questions you may have about HIV, AIDS, or the test.

After this, a lab technician will draw a vial of blood from your arm. This is done by tying a piece of rubber tubing tightly around your upper arm so that the veins in your arm stand out a little. The technician will then wipe your arm with alcohol, usually near the bend in your elbow or near a vein in your hand. A needle is then inserted into a vein and a vial of blood is drawn. While there is a quick jab when the needle enters your arm, the procedure does not hurt, and it takes only a few seconds. There is no danger of infection from the needle because it is thrown away after it is used. The technician may also draw a second vial of blood (the needle does not have to be removed; the syringe is just changed) if you are being tested for other things. For example, some cities have had recent outbreaks of syphilis and ask people taking the HIV test if they will agree to be tested for syphilis as well.

Your blood sample is then labeled with your name (if you are being tested through a doctor or private testing center) or your identification number and sent to a lab that specializes in performing antibody tests. The lab will first perform the ELISA test described in question 84. If your blood sample tests positive after the ELISA test, it will be retested with the Western blot test. If this test is positive, a further antigen or viral culture test may also be done. If these additional tests are also positive, your test result is reported to the place where you were tested as being positive for HIV.

If your ELISA test is negative or **inconclusive** (meaning that a definite result was not given), the test will be run again. If it is still negative or inconclusive, these results are reported to the place where you were tested.

Because there are so many people being tested for HIV, it will take about two or three weeks for the place where you were tested to get your results. Depending on where you went for your test, you will either be called with the results or, more likely, asked to come in to get your results in person. You will sit down with the counselor who talked to you before the test. She or he will tell you whether your test was negative, positive, or inconclusive.

86.
What does a positive HIV test result mean?

A positive result to an AIDS test tells you that your immune system has produced antibodies to HIV, the virus that causes AIDS. It does *not* mean that you have AIDS. It means that you have been infected by the virus that causes AIDS. While one in three people who test positive for HIV develops an AIDS-related disease within five years of diagnosis, it has not yet been determined how many people who test positive will actually develop full-blown AIDS.

87.

What does a negative or inconclusive HIV test result mean?

A negative test result tells you either that your immune system has not yet produced antibodies to the AIDS virus or that you are not infected with HIV. An inconclusive result means that the test was not able to determine whether or not there were antibodies to HIV in your blood. In the case of an inconclusive result, another blood sample is taken, and the test is repeated using fresh blood.

88.

Isn't it better not to know if you have HIV?

Some people think that it is easier not to know if they are infected. Their attitude seems to be, "If I have HIV I'm going to die, so I'd rather not know." This is a very dangerous attitude. New treatments for people with HIV are being developed, and the earlier treatment starts, the longer a person may live. If you find out very early on that you have been infected by HIV, you can begin treatment sooner. Not knowing also puts other people in danger. If you are participating in risky behavior and there is the possibility that you are HIV-positive, you are putting other people at risk as well.

89.
Can an HIV test result be wrong?

There is a chance that a test result may be incorrect, but it is very unlikely. If a test result is incorrect, it is usually what is called a **false-positive**. This means that a person who is really uninfected by HIV gets a positive test result. For people who do not participate in high-risk activities, the chance of this happening is about 1 in 10,000. For people who have participated in high-risk behavior, a positive result on an HIV test is correct 99 times out of 100.

The least-likely type of incorrect test result is called a **false-negative**. This means that a person who really is infected with HIV tests negative for antibodies to the virus. This usually occurs when a test is given within the window period. For example, a person may have been infected with HIV in mid-March and been tested in early April. During that period, the body may not have had time to manufacture enough antibodies to the virus to be detected by a test. In that case, the person's test would come back negative, even though she really was infected.

90.
How often should I be tested for HIV?

If you have not engaged in high-risk activity, you will probably be safe getting tested only once, because the chance that you are infected is very small. If you have engaged in risky activity, it is wise to be tested several times. Because mistakes can happen with testing, most testing centers suggest that people who have participated in high-risk activities get tested once and then again after six months of not participating in any high-risk activity. If the results of these tests are the same after repeated testings, the chance of the results being incorrect is almost zero.

91.
Why do some people say that there should be mandatory HIV testing?

Mandatory testing, testing that is required by law, is a controversial subject, especially where AIDS is concerned. Some people feel that everyone should be tested for HIV for the good of the public. They think that people have the right to know if another person has a disease that can be transmitted. Other people argue that only people in certain professions, such as doctors, nurses, and dentists, should be tested to protect their patients. Others believe that all prisoners, pregnant women, and people applying for marriage licenses should be tested.

But mandatory testing poses a lot of problems. Who decides what groups should be tested? Who is told the results of the testing? How does mandatory testing protect the public from getting HIV?

People still discriminate against people with HIV, and often treat those who they think might be infected differently. HIV-positive people may lose their jobs and their homes because people are afraid of them. And many insurance companies are reluctant to provide coverage for HIV-positive people or people they think may be HIV-positive because of the high costs involved in fighting the AIDS virus.

Because there is still a lot of misinformation about how HIV is spread, many people would be discriminated against simply out of ignorance. And because a certain percentage of antibody tests are false-positive, a number of people who weren't infected would test positive. Even if a person were HIV-positive, making this information public could be devastating.

There are some agencies, like the military, the Job Corps, and the Peace Corps, that do require HIV testing as part of their admission procedures, and they do not admit people who test positive for HIV. Whether this is a good idea or not is a matter of personal opinion. In addition, all donated blood and organs are tested for the AIDS virus, and the donors are informed if the test is positive.

92.
What do I do if I am HIV-positive?

If your test result is positive, your doctor or the counselor at the clinic where you had your test should refer
you to places that specialize in helping people with
HIV infection. The most important thing for you to realize is that your life is not over just because you test
positive for HIV. The young people in the interviews in
this book have all been living with HIV, some for many
years. There are many organizations across the country
that specialize in helping people who test positive for
HIV get information about treatment programs. There
are also many support groups for people with HIV and
AIDS, some of which are designed specifically for
teenagers. You can find some of these groups listed in
the Resource Guide in this book.

One thing you *must* do if you test positive for
the AIDS virus is go back and contact as many people
that you might have infected as you can. These people
have no idea that you are infected with HIV and may
be passing the virus on to others. While it may be hard
to tell them that you are infected, it is important to let
them know that they may have come into contact with
HIV. If you do not feel comfortable doing this, some
agencies will contact potentially infected partners for
you.

93.
What is done to treat people with HIV and AIDS?

When talking about treating people with AIDS, you are actually talking about treating two different things: the AIDS virus and the AIDS-related diseases. Each of the AIDS-related diseases can be diagnosed and combatted in many ways. There are many treatments to fight AIDS-related diseases such as *pneumocystis carinii* pneumonia and Kaposi's sarcoma, for example.

But the AIDS virus itself is different. HIV invades cells in many different parts of the body, including the digestive system, the brain, the sexual organs, and the immune system. Getting rid of the virus completely would mean destroying all the cells infected with the virus. Since these cells are necessary for life, doctors cannot do this.

Despite this problem, there are treatments for people with AIDS. The two drugs most commonly used to treat AIDS are **AZT** and **ddl**. AZT, the chemical name for the drug zidovudine, was until 1991 the only drug approved by the Food and Drug Administration (FDA) for the treatment of AIDS. AZT is an **antiviral**. An antiviral is a drug that prevents a virus from working and that stops the virus from multiplying within healthy cells. In the case of AZT, this means slowing down the rate at which HIV replicates itself within T-cells and other cells. This does not destroy HIV, but it does slow down the spread of the virus, which keeps the immune system working for as long as possible and helps prevent the onset of opportunistic infections.

When AZT was first developed, it was given only to people who were in the later stages of AIDS. Then it was discovered that giving AZT to people when they were first diagnosed would help slow down the rate at which their immune systems deteriorated. Many people thought AZT was a miracle drug. It prevented many of the opportunistic diseases common with HIV infection, and it helped people feel better, have fewer fevers, and gain weight.

There are, however, several problems with AZT. Its effects last for only about four hours, so it has to be taken in liquid or pill form many times each day. If a person misses one dose, the work done by the AZT will start to wear off. AZT also causes side effects in some people who take it. These can range from general nausea to serious problems with the liver. Besides affecting HIV, AZT can also prevent action in some healthy cells, and this may cause other side effects. Finally, AZT is very expensive. It can cost a person hundreds of dollars a month to stay on AZT. If someone does not have insurance or insurance does not cover everything, that person will have to pay enormous amounts of money for treatment.

In October 1991, the FDA approved a second drug, didanosine, for the treatment of AIDS. Didanosine, or ddI, is also an antiviral that slows down the rate of replication of HIV within healthy cells. DdI is generally given to people who do not respond well to AZT or to people who are in the later stages of HIV infection. Like AZT, ddI can cause side effects, such as nerve damage and damage to the pancreas.

Currently, ddI and AZT are the only drugs officially approved for fighting the AIDS virus directly. There are, however, many treatments that are used by people with HIV infection to fight their disease, ranging from vitamin therapy to herbal healing to the use of crystals. No one knows for sure if these kinds of alternative therapies actually physically help a person with AIDS, but they may help a person deal mentally and emotionally with HIV infection.

94.
Who can I talk to about HIV and AIDS?

Because AIDS is a disease that affects so many people, most cities have established counseling centers that specialize in answering HIV questions. In addition, there are many groups around the country that specialize in offering groups for young people who want to know more about HIV and AIDS. You can find them in the phone book, or look in the back of this book to find centers in your area.

95.
Why do some people say that people with AIDS deserve the disease?

AIDS can be a very frightening disease, and many people find it hard to talk about AIDS because it means talking about sex and drugs, things that we are usually taught to be afraid or ashamed of. People who say that anyone deserves AIDS are simply ignorant and afraid. They think that only drug addicts, people who have a lot of indiscriminate sex, and other people they consider "bad" get AIDS, and they like to think that they are better than people who participate in high-risk behavior. They also think that they don't know anyone affected by AIDS and that AIDS will never affect them. They are wrong. Anyone can get AIDS, and almost everyone knows of somebody that has been affected by HIV.

People with AIDS are not bad people, and they are not being "punished" for anything they did. They are people who have contracted a disease. AIDS does not pick certain people to infect because of who they are. It can infect captains of baseball teams, farmers, ministers, firefighters, models, class valedictorians, or anyone else. You do not have to be a drug addict to get AIDS; you only have to use an infected needle once. You don't have to have sex with a lot of people to get AIDS; you only have to pick the wrong person once. The only people who should be ashamed are the ones who say that anyone deserves to have AIDS.

96.
Someone I know has AIDS, and now my friends don't want me to talk to him. How can I tell them it's okay?

The best way to deal with people who don't understand AIDS is to give them the facts. Give them books like this one, or pamphlets from AIDS organizations. Remember that they are afraid of AIDS because they don't understand what it's all about. Help them to learn more about HIV and AIDS. As more and more people begin to understand AIDS, the fear surrounding the disease will go away.

97.
My brother is HIV-positive, and I'm afraid to tell anyone. How can I deal with my feelings?

For everyone who has HIV disease, there are fathers, sisters, lovers, brothers, friends, and mothers who are dealing with that person's illness. These people all need to be able to talk about what they are feeling. There are many organizations around the country that help the families and friends of HIV-positive people and people with AIDS deal with their feelings. The best way to deal with your feelings about AIDS is to talk about them with other people who have experienced the same thing. The worst thing you can do is bottle all your feelings up inside and pretend that nothing is wrong.

98.
My six-year-old sister wants to know about AIDS. What should I tell her?

AIDS is in the news a lot these days, and children are becoming aware of it at a very early age. Many young children are frightened because they don't understand AIDS. They think they can get it like they get a cold, or that they can get it from a blood test. They need to be told that these things are not dangerous. Young children do not have to be told all the details involved with sex in order to understand AIDS. Telling them that AIDS is a disease that people get by doing certain things is usually enough. Children really want to know how they *can't* get AIDS. They should be reassured that they do not have to worry about blood tests, or having their teeth cleaned, or of people with AIDS sneezing near them, playing with them, or kissing them.

99.
What should I say when someone tells me she or he is infected with HIV?

When a friend tells you that she or he has been infected with HIV, that person has chosen to trust you with very important information. Unless your friend asks you to, do not tell anyone else about his or her condition. Because of ignorance about AIDS, discrimination still exists, and even though *you* have the facts, not everyone will respond kindly.

One of the biggest problems faced by people with AIDS is the psychological stress of having to tell people that they are infected and worrying about whether people will reject them. This can often be harder than dealing with the disease itself. The most important thing you can do for a friend who tells you he or she is HIV-positive is to tell your friend, "I am here for you when you need me."

You must also learn to understand your friend's disease. Find out all you can about AIDS so that you can recognize when your friend needs rest or needs help with something. This might mean staying in on a Friday night and watching television because your friend is tired, when you would rather have gone to a movie or gone dancing. It might mean attending support groups with your friend or going along on visits to the doctor.

This does not mean that you have to treat your friend like an invalid or a dying patient. You do not have to always ask if your friend is all right or be a nurse. The person is still the same person you loved before she or he was infected. You can still hug and kiss your friend and share food and drinks. Your friend will still enjoy ball games and fishing trips, concerts and shopping, and will still want to do these things with you.

100.
What can I do about AIDS?

Teenagers probably have the biggest chance to make an impact on the AIDS crisis because they are able to talk to one another about things that they might have difficulty talking to adults about. Teenagers are also at an age where they are making decisions about sex and drugs. If they can be taught to make responsible decisions at an early age, young people will make a big difference in who becomes infected with HIV in the years ahead.

The most powerful tool in the fight against AIDS is education. If you know the facts about what AIDS is, how it is transmitted, and how to prevent it, you are way ahead of most people. Start by telling your friends what you have learned. Tell them about using condoms and cleaning needles. Teach them not to be afraid of people with AIDS. As more people learn the facts about AIDS, their fears about the disease will disappear.

You can also help by starting an AIDS information center at your school. Many schools are adding AIDS education to their course of study, and many school health offices are setting up areas especially for AIDS information. Direct other students to these areas or suggest books and pamphlets that might make good additions to your school's library or AIDS education program.

Another way you can help in the fight against AIDS is by inviting people to come speak to your school about the disease. There are many groups across the United States that will provide speakers for free or for little charge to schools. Some of these organizations include teenagers who have been infected with the AIDS virus. Look in the resource section of this book for groups in your area.

One of the most rewarding ways you can get involved in the AIDS crisis is by volunteering to work for an AIDS-related organization. A lot of the work in the battle against AIDS is done by volunteers, and almost every city in the country has an organization that works in some way with AIDS. Many of these volunteer activities require no special skills or training. Others will train you to do whatever they need. You don't have to know everything about AIDS or know someone with AIDS to be a volunteer.

Volunteer groups need people to do everything from work in the office for an hour or two a week, helping with filing or mailings, to becoming a buddy to someone with AIDS. A buddy is someone who visits a person with AIDS and helps with shopping, taking care of pets, and other errands, or just sits and talks or reads to her or him. You can also volunteer to work on a telephone hotline, answering people's questions about AIDS and HIV, or work for a group that prepares meals for people with AIDS. You might want to join a group that offers peer counseling, where you speak to people your own age about AIDS.

Perhaps the most important thing you can do is to show compassion for people with HIV disease and for the people affected by their illness. Think about how you would feel if you or someone you cared about were HIV-positive or had AIDS. When you hear people telling jokes about people with AIDS or making remarks about someone with HIV infection, let them know that that is not acceptable behavior. Wear a button that shows your dedication to the fight against AIDS, or a red ribbon to remember all the women and men who have died from HIV disease. If someone asks you what the button or ribbon means, take time to tell them.

Finally, you can support artists who donate money to AIDS organizations. Many musicians, including R.E.M., Elton John, Queen, the B-52s, and especially Madonna, all support the fight against AIDS and donate money from record sales to various organizations. Others, such as Dee-Lite and Salt-n-Pepa, have recorded songs with safer-sex messages.

Whatever you decide to do makes a difference. One person can do a great deal of good, so don't think that just because you are young, you can't volunteer. All across the United States, young people are stuffing envelopes, handing out condoms, educating people about AIDS, marching for increased AIDS-research funding, writing letters to the government, and contributing to the fight against the AIDS epidemic.

Justin

In 1980, when he was ten years old, Justin Early found himself a runaway on the streets of Seattle. With nowhere else to go, he was soon selling his body for sex to survive and to buy the drugs he had become addicted to.

For the next 11 years, Justin lived the life of a street kid, a life shared by thousands of other young runaways in the United States. In 1991, while living in San Francisco, Justin developed an abscess on his leg that required hospitalization. In the hospital he was tested for HIV, and the test was positive.

Justin went to live at Walden House, a group home in San Francisco that has a program for HIV-positive people. A year later, at 22, he has a full-time job, is drug and alcohol free, and is looking forward to the future.

Many of you reading Justin's story are going to think that it is nothing you can relate to, that you could never end up in his situation. But the reality is that every year many young people run away from home for various reasons. Some are being abused physically or emotionally and see it as the only way out. Others just don't get along with their parents, and run away hoping to make things better.

Many of these runaways end up as street kids, often turning to prostitution and drug use. Increasingly, these young people are becoming HIV-positive. Recent studies estimate that up to 25% of all street kids are carrying the AIDS virus, and most don't even know it because there are very few facilities for runaway and homeless people to learn about HIV and AIDS and get tested.

As you read Justin's story, remember that there are a lot of other young people out there who are in the same position he was in. What happened to him could happen to any of us.

What made you leave home?

I was having a lot of problems with my parents. We were fighting a lot, and it finally just got to be too much.

So you ran away?

I ran away and went to a police station in Seattle. They took me to a foster home and I met up with another kid who was older than me. He asked me if I wanted to run away and go down to the streets. I had heard a lot about the streets and I found it very interesting because I knew it was wrong.

Because it went completely against your upbringing?

It felt good to me. It was a good way to get back at my parents. So I went. I made it down to the street one afternoon and I started meeting people. I was the youngest, the cute little ten-year-old that everybody wanted to take care of, so I won a lot of hearts.

How did you get into prostitution?

All my friends were doing it and they set me up in it. A lot of my tricks [men who pay for sex] were interested in me because I was so young. So I started doing that.

How did the drugs start?

We had a little clique of kids who lived down there. And they started doing dope.

Did your parents know you were on the streets?

Yes, I kept in contact with my mother. I even went back home a couple times. But I would get real fidgety there and run back down to the streets and start shooting drugs again.

Did your parents know you were prostituting?

I was arrested for prostitution when I was 11. That's when my father quit talking to me. My name wasn't in the papers, but the incident was, and they knew it was me because the Youth Authority called them and said, "Your son has been arrested for prostitution." They came downtown looking for me. There was a place called the Doughnut Shop and I was sitting in there one night and my father walked in and said, "You're coming home." And I said, "No, I'm not." And the guy behind the counter, he knew what kind of problems I had at home, so he said, "You're not taking this kid anywhere, so take your hands off him." Then there was a brawl with this guy and a couple other people jumped in to get my father off me and I ran out the door and went to my street-sister's apartment.

What did you do then?

I went back to the streets. I was kicking it with the drug crowd downtown, pulling tricks, shooting dope in bathrooms and using toilet water to shoot dope, even my spit if I had to. And I had some friends that I had met, kids that were shooting, so I would buy from them and I'd be out in the snow shooting dope and the dope would be freezing up in the works. It was bad.

How long did this last?
In July of 1989, while I was in jail for stealing a car, I got really sick. I was bleeding internally and started showing purple spots all over my skin. So I went into the hospital and they ran some AIDS tests. They all came back negative. They gave me a transfusion and put me back in jail. When I got out I called this guy I had met in San Francisco during the summer. I told him I wanted to leave Seattle because the drugs were really bad and I needed to leave because all I knew were drug people. So he put me on a bus, took me to his house. This lasted until a friend of mine stole some video equipment from this guy. Then he kicked me out. He drove me downtown and dropped me off. I started doing a lot of heroin and coke. This was the end of September, and I had just turned 20. In November I was arrested for possession of cocaine. I got out at the end of December. On Christmas Day I was out looking for dope. I didn't have anywhere to go. I didn't call my family or anything because I was so torn up. I had scabs all over my face, blood all over my clothes, my hair was long and greasy, and I had tracks all over my arms. Then in January, the day the Gulf War started, I got on a bus and went back to Seattle because my mother had called and said that my brother was in the hospital with a malignant brain tumor. That same day my grandfather died. So I got to my parents' house and my father wouldn't let me go see my brother.

I decided to go down and start shooting dope on the streets again. I hooked up with my old friends, started turning tricks. Finally, a friend and I stole a car and drove back to San Francisco.

What happened once you got back?
The first night we were back, we went and got some coke. I went into a bathroom and shot it in my ankle because the veins in my arms were shot. I didn't think I missed or anything, but it was a little bit sore. Then about 24 hours later I couldn't walk. I had to call an ambulance to come get me. They came and took me to the hospital. While I was in the hospital a man named Scott Walker who worked at an alcohol and substance abuse program came up and asked if I would take an AIDS test. I said I would, and they took blood. But then I got kicked out of the hospital for smoking in the hallway.

So how did you get your results?
I was doing methadone detox. I went to the place where Scott Walker worked to get methadone, and one day he said, "You know, you've missed two appointments to get your results." I was really scared because I didn't want to get the results. I had this feeling that they would be positive. So Scott said, "I don't think you should get your dose of methadone until you go and get your results." I said, "I'll make you a deal. You give me the dose and I'll go get the results." So they gave me the dose and I went. The lady couldn't find the results because I had missed two appointments. She finally found them and put me in a room. Then she sat down and told me I was positive.

How did you react?

At first I was in shock. Tears came to my eyes and everything shut down. This was April 11, 1991. I went back to Scott's office and said, "Scott, I'm positive and I don't know what I'm going to do." What I did know was that if I went out and started shooting dope again I'd die quick, my body wouldn't take it. Scott gave me the card of a lady who worked at Walden House, so I went down there. They had just started this new program for people who are HIV-positive, and I was the perfect candidate for it because I had just tested HIV-positive, I didn't know what I was going to do, and I was homeless. But before I could enter I had to go to jail because there was a warrant out for my arrest for an old auto theft charge. On May 29, 1991, I got out and I went to Walden House. I've been here ever since.

Have you determined when you were infected?

In fall of 1989 I was living with a guy and shooting drugs with him. He had AIDS. I would go and buy the dope and come home and split it with him. We would use the same spoon and sometimes the same needle. Once in a while I would use bleach. I thought I wouldn't get it because I used bleach once in a while. But I was wrong. He was really sick. He had Kaposi's sarcoma all over his face. But I rationalized it. I didn't see it. I didn't want to see it. I thought I was indestructible.

I think most kids think that.

I know I did. That's why I stayed on the street when I was a kid. That's why I didn't listen to anybody. Everything that they were telling me was happening wasn't going to happen to me. I wasn't going to be homeless. I was never going to get strung out on drugs. And God forbid that I was ever going to be HIV-positive or get AIDS. It just wasn't going to happen.

When you were prostituting and shooting drugs, did you ever think about what your future would be like?

I wouldn't look ahead. Sometimes I would say, "I'm going to get into school and get a job before it's too late. I'll get out." But I kept putting it off and putting it off. I just never took the steps to do it. The drugs became more important—that carefree lifestyle became more important.

Are you looking ahead now?

I think I might want to go into accounting, go to college. I was on AZT for a while and it was very toxic for me. I couldn't take it. I was really scared. I didn't know what I was going to do if I couldn't take AZT. I thought my life was over. Then I ran across these Chinese herbs. I'm on those now and I feel wonderful. Absolutely great. I don't think I was meant to be on AZT. I think the herbs will keep me going and whatever happens happens. And hopefully something good will happen. I like to think I'll be here for the cure. The way things are going, they say there could be a cure within five years. I don't know if it's true, but it's something to look forward to. I know I can make it for another five years easy. Right now I'm asymptomatic. I do acupuncture every three weeks and I'm in therapy.

You're going for the alternative therapies?
They're working for me like they work for a lot of other people. I've noticed that people with positive attitudes who take the herbs, do the acupuncture and the stress reduction make it a lot longer. But the people with negative attitudes that sit around saying "I'm sick" are the ones who get sick.

Do you think much about what could happen?
No. I get scared more when it comes to thinking about resocializing and meeting somebody. There are a lot of people that are attracted to me that I'm attracted to, but I get really scared because I don't want to tell them that I'm positive and watch them run away. Even if I get into a relationship and it works out, eventually something may happen. I have to look at the cons as well as the pros. Things aren't always positive in life. Anything can happen.

How has your attitude about life changed since you tested positive?
It made me look at my life and see that it could end. I'm not indestructible anymore, and I realized that I needed to start making changes. What I see is that people with positive outlooks are making it. And that's where I want

to be. I want to make it. When I first got here to Walden House my attitude was, "I'm just going to die, so let me have my way." I played on that big time. But they said, "No, you can't think that way because the only way you're going to die is if you let yourself die. Start taking care of yourself now. Change your attitude." When I came here I had had so many years of no structure, of selling my ass on the street and shooting drugs, that I didn't know anything else. I think it all started to turn around when I got my high-school equivalency degree. That was my big accomplishment. Also, I worked my way up to being the facility manager's assistant here, and everybody looked up to me. I am a role model. That is great because I'm young, I'm HIV-positive, and I'm gay. Each one of those categories has a very low success rate, and I'm all three and I still made it.

You've really turned youself around this past year.
I had to. I had to get out of all of it—the drugs, the alcohol, the prostitution, the manipulation.

Do you think you would have done it if you hadn't tested positive?
No. I wouldn't have because I would have been indestructible still. This has been a real reality check.

Are you angry about everything you've gone through?
I've dealt with a lot of anger. There was nobody I was more angry at than myself, for letting it go so long. I did

what's called beating a pillow, which is hitting a pillow with a bat to get your anger out. And I beat the hell out of this big huge pillow and I just cried and I was so angry that I beat and I beat and I got out a lot of that anger. There were lots of feelings toward my family that led me to the streets and kept me on the streets. There were a lot of things I went through on the streets that I had to process. So when I got off the drugs, these things started coming up, like how much my father hated me and how I'm HIV-positive and gay and how the tricks on the streets made me feel dirty. And all this stuff started coming up and I dealt with it and got rid of it and was able to live again.

What should young people know about HIV?

That it's out there. Your best friend could have it and not know about it. They could show no symptoms, look healthier than ever and still have it. And it only takes one time. One time, and that's it. Just like getting pregnant. And you're not going to know about it for six weeks to six months. It's there, especially in young people because they're indestructible. Like I was—indestructible. That's why they're out there taking chances, and that's why so many of them are getting it today. They need to start finding out what's going on.

When you feel bad about yourself is it harder to care?

That's how I felt when I was shooting dope with this guy who gave me HIV. I didn't care. I knew he had it, and I didn't care. I didn't see a week ahead of me. I was living for today, to get my dope today, to shoot my dope today. And that was it.

Do the kids on the street talk about AIDS?
They talk about people they know who have it. But they're not going to get it. They talk about how they're all negative, convincing themselves that it's true.

What do these street kids need to know?
That if they don't get it together they're going to get AIDS. People who think they're not going to get it are just the ones who are going to get it. And nothing is worth getting it for. They need to take a risk on themselves—take the risk of getting it together and doing what they need to do to get off the streets. They've been shooting dope and pulling tricks for so long that that's all they know. They know they can always go back to that. Why not get your life together for a minute and see what it's like? They're scared that if something goes right for two seconds they won't know what to do. Just take that risk and see what being productive means and being happy means. Sure, I was happy on the streets. I was happy when I got twenty dollars from a trick. I was happy when I could go to the dope man with some money and get a hit. But that's not happy.

And now?
Now I can look in the mirror and say, "Hey, you're all right."

Do your parents know that you're HIV-positive?

I told my mom. She just kind of took some deep breaths. She works for the state, and they teach them about AIDS, so she knows what it's about. Then she started crying. She started crying really bad.

Does it hurt that you can't count on them?

It does. It does a lot. But I have real good friends. I'm in a support group. I've met some other people who are HIV-positive, and some who aren't. It helps having other people my own age to talk to.

Do you ever feel like someone's taken something from you?

Sometimes, but then I stop myself. Whatever's going to happen is going to happen. I have today. Just make today okay. And that kind of positive attitude can take me many years down the line. Sometimes I wonder why I should go through school and get a job when I'm just going to get sick and die, won't be able to go to work half the time because I'll be home sick in bed. But then I realize that that's not true. If I can keep my stress level down, stay off drugs, quit smoking, I can stay well for a long time. And I'm real hopeful that they will have some kind of a cure.

Are there times when it's too much?

Once in a while, mostly around the relationship issue. But basically I still feel indestructible, although now it's in a positive way. I'm not going to let this thing kill me. I'm just not. That's the kind of attitude I'm trying to keep. And hopefully it will work. And if it doesn't, oh well. As long as I'm not in a lot of pain. I don't want to die in a lot of pain.

What's your advice to kids out there who feel like they aren't worth taking care of?

Go get help. Reach out. Get into a program. You have to take a look at yourself and break down to the point where you can start building up again. And stay away from all the people you knew, no matter how close you were. I have a lot of people that I was close to, but I can't contact them because they use, and that's too dangerous for me. I can't put myself into that situation.

What do you think about people who say that you got what you deserve for doing the things you did?

It's an easy way out for a lot of people to not see the pain that other people are going through. They're running from their feelings of fear. They don't want to feel anything because it's painful, and who wants to feel pain? Fear, sorrow, anger—those are all real deep feelings, and people don't want to deal with them. The easy way out is to call AIDS God's punishment and let everyone with AIDS die. They don't want to see people in all that pain.

RESOURCE
guide

The following section contains information on organizations that have been set up to help answer any questions that you might have about HIV and AIDS or other sexually transmitted diseases. Some are hotlines, telephone services that you can call with questions, or to get referrals for various services such as counseling and medical treatment, or to get the names of places that can provide speakers for your school. Others are organizations that you can write or go to for information about a variety of subjects, ranging from birth control to AIDS education, to help in dealing with issues of sexual identity.

The hotlines and the organizations listed are not the only ones in the country. They are major groups from various areas across the United States that have proven to be reliable sources of information. If you call one of the places listed in this guide, people there will be able to refer you to organizations in your area that can help you.

Most of the telephone numbers listed in this resource guide are 800 numbers, which means that they are toll-free. If you call them, you will not have to pay for the call, and the call will not appear on your telephone bill. Phone numbers that do not begin with 1-800 are not toll-free. There is a charge for calling these numbers, and they will appear on your phone bill.

NATIONAL AIDS HOTLINE

If you have questions about HIV and AIDS, you can easily get the information you need by calling the National AIDS Hotline. The National AIDS Hotline is operated by the Centers for Disease Control and is the most reliable source of information about HIV and AIDS. The counselors who answer the phone have many resources available to them and can answer questions about HIV and AIDS as well as refer you to organizations in your area that deal with whatever issues you are concerned with.

National AIDS Hotline
1-800-342-AIDS
1-800-342-2437
24 hours a day, every day

National AIDS Hotline in Spanish
1-800-344-SIDA
1-800-344-7432
8:00 A.M.–2:00 A.M. every day

National AIDS Hotline for the Hearing Impaired
1-800-243-7889
10:00 A.M.–10:00 P.M. Monday-Friday

NATIONAL AIDS CLEARINGHOUSE

Another organization run by the Centers for Disease Control is the National AIDS Clearinghouse. The Clearinghouse offers printed information on HIV and AIDS to schools or groups involved in AIDS education. If your school has an AIDS education program, the Clearinghouse can offer help in obtaining quality materials. You should not, however, call them if you have basic questions about HIV and AIDS. For answers to your questions, you should call one of the hotlines listed on page 166.

National AIDS Clearinghouse
P.O. Box 6003
Rockville, MD 20850
1-800-458-5231

STATE HOTLINES

While it is advisable to call the National AIDS Hotline for answers to your questions about HIV and AIDS, you might want to call the AIDS Hotline in your state for information on organizations in your specific area that deal with HIV and AIDS-related issues. Below is a state-by-state listing of AIDS information numbers that you can call if the National AIDS Hotline does not have information about your area.

Alabama	1-800-228-0469
Alaska	1-800-478-2437
Arizona	1-800-334-1540
Arkansas	1-800-445-7720
California	
Northern	1-800-367-2437
Southern	1-800-922-2437
Colorado	1-800-252-2437
Connecticut	1-800-842-2437
Delaware	1-800-422-0429
District of Columbia	1-202-332-2437
Florida	1-800-352-2437
Georgia	1-800-551-2728
Hawaii	1-808-922-1313
Idaho	1-800-677-2437
Illinois	1-800-782-0423
Indiana	1-800-848-2437
Iowa	1-800-445-2437
Kansas	1-800-232-0040
Kentucky	1-800-654-2437
Louisiana	1-800-992-4379
Maine	1-800-851-2437

Maryland	1-800-638-6252
Massachusetts	1-800-235-2331
Michigan	1-800-872-2437
Mississippi	1-800-537-0851
Minnesota	1-800-248-2437
Missouri	1-800-533-2437
Montana	1-800-233-6668
Nebraska	1-800-782-2437
Nevada	1-702-687-4804
New Hampshire	1-800-872-8909
New Jersey	1-800-624-2377
New Mexico	1-800-545-2437
New York	1-800-541-2437
North Carolina	1-800-535-2437
North Dakota	1-800-472-2180
Ohio	1-800-332-2437
Oklahoma	1-800-522-9054
Oregon	1-800-777-2437
Pennsylvania	1-800-662-6080
Puerto Rico	1-809-765-1010
Rhode Island	1-800-726-3010
South Carolina	1-800-322-2437
South Dakota	1-800-592-1861
Tennessee	1-800-525-2437
Texas	1-800-248-1091
Utah	1-801-538-6094
Vermont	1-800-882-2437
Virginia	1-800-533-4148
Virgin Islands	1-809-773-1311
Washington	1-800-272-2437
West Virginia	1-800-642-8244
Wisconsin	1-800-334-2437
Wyoming	1-800-327-3577

HOTLINES FOR YOUNG PEOPLE

In addition to the National AIDS Hotline, there are many hotlines that have been set up specifically for young people. These hotlines offer advice and information on a variety of subjects, including HIV and AIDS. Some hotlines are designed for anyone who has questions. Others have been established for homeless teens; runaways; or lesbian, gay, and bisexual teens.

Covenant House
1-800-999-9999

Also called the Nine Line, this 24-hour number will connect the caller with Covenant House, an organization with offices in many different parts of the country, including New York City, New Orleans, and Houston. Covenant House offers services for young people of all kinds, including runaway, homeless, substance addicted, abused, and suicidal youth.

Gay and Lesbian Youth Hotline
1-800-347-8336
Thursday-Sunday 7:00 A.M.-11:00 P.M. Eastern time

Sponsored by the Indianapolis Youth Group, the hotline offers crisis counseling and referrals to young people dealing with all aspects of sexual identity. They will also refer you to groups in your specific area.

National Gay Task Force Crisis Line
1-800-221-7044

A hotline based in New York City that offers counseling and referrals to lesbian and gay people. Open Monday–Friday, 5:00 P.M.–10:00 P.M. and Saturday from 1:00 P.M.– 5:00 P.M.

National Runaway Hotline
1-800-231-6946

A 24-hour hotline that provides information and referral services for shelter, counseling, and medical and legal services, as well as transportation home for runaway teens anywhere in the country. The hotline also provides a confidential message-relay service between runaways and their families.

National Runaway Switchboard
1-800-621-4000

A 24-hour crisis hotline for runaway and homeless young people and their families. The hotline provides information and referrals for housing, medical services, and counseling, and message delivery between youth and their families. The switchboard also provides crisis intervention and suicide counseling serving the entire United States.

Teens Teaching AIDS Prevention

1-800-234-TEEN

A switchboard operated by teenagers who have been trained to answer questions about HIV and AIDS. It is open Monday–Saturday, 4:00 P.M.–8:00 P.M.

Youth Development International

1-800-HIT-HOME

A 24-hour hotline that offers counseling and referrals to teenagers dealing with a variety of issues, including substance abuse, homelessness, sexual abuse, pregnancy, and HIV and AIDS.

GENERAL ORGANIZATIONS

The following organizations offer information on a variety of topics, including HIV and AIDS. Some provide counseling and speakers for groups. Others provide printed information about HIV and AIDS. This is not meant to be an exhaustive list. It is simply a list of major organizations throughout the country that are good places to start if you are looking for more information. These organizations will have the names of many more places that you can go to.

Adolescent AIDS Program
Montefiore Medical Center
Albert Einstein College of Medicine
111 East 210th Street
Bronx, NY 10467
(718) 920-2179

A special program developed to help people between the ages of 12 and 21. It offers medical services, including HIV testing and counseling, and printed information about HIV and AIDS.

AID Atlanta
1132 West Peachtree Street NW
Atlanta, GA 30309
(404) 872-0600

An organization for people with HIV or AIDS. AID Atlanta offers a buddy program, medical referrals, HIV and AIDS counseling, and testing information. They also provide a training program for teens who want to become involved in counseling other teens.

AIDS Action Committee
131 Clarendon Street
Boston, MA 02116
(617) 437-6200

An AIDS-services organization offering counseling and support groups, financial assistance, housing and meal support, and a buddy program for people with AIDS.

American Indian Health Care Association
245 East Sixth Street
Suite 499
St. Paul, MN 55101
(612) 293-0233

An organization dedicated to studying health issues in the American Indian community. The National Urban Indian AIDS Information and Education Project provides education about HIV and AIDS to Native Americans.

American Red Cross
National Headquarters
HIV/AIDS Project for Youth
1709 New York Avenue
Suite 100
Washington, D.C. 20006
(202) 662-1580

A national organization offering information on a variety of health-care issues. The HIV/AIDS Project for Youth provides information on AIDS education to groups working with young people.

Bay Area Young Positives

c/o Julie Graham
4316 California Street
San Francisco, CA 94118
(415) 386-4615

A group in the San Francisco Bay area that offers peer counseling and support groups for HIV-positive people in any stage of infection. Bay Area Young Positives will provide speakers for groups interested in learning more about HIV and AIDS and what it is like to live with AIDS. They are currently developing support groups specifically for Asian, Hispanic, and African-American HIV-positive young people.

Center for Population Options

1025 Vermont Avenue NW
Suite 210
Washington, D.C. 20005
(202) 347-5700

The Center for Population Options (CPO) is a nonprofit educational organization dedicated to improving the quality of life for adolescents by improving decision making through life-planning and sexuality-education programs. For further information about CPO's Adolescent AIDS and HIV Prevention Initiative, write to the above address.

Gay Men's Health Crisis

129 West 20th Street
New York, NY 10011
(212) 807-6664
(212) 807-6655 hotline

Originally established to meet the needs of people with
AIDS in the lesbian and gay community, GMHC now
offers a range of services to all people with HIV infection
and their friends and families, including testing
information, buddy programs, a hotline, legal services,
and social events. They have an extensive volunteer
program and hold frequent training sessions for those
interested in becoming volunteers.

Hispanic AIDS Forum

Manhattan Office
121 Avenue of the Americas
Room 505
New York, NY 10013
(212) 966-6336
(212) 966-6662 bilingual hotline

Queens Office
74-09 37th Avenue
Room 400
Jackson Heights, NY 11372
(718) 803-2766

An organization serving the Latino community with
offices in Manhattan and Queens. The Forum offers
bilingual services including seminars, workshops, AIDS
outreach and information programs, counseling, support

groups, and medical referrals for lesbian and gay people as well as for substance abusers and homeless people. They will also arrange for speakers to come talk to schools and groups interested in AIDS education.

The National Association of People With AIDS

1413 K Street NW
10th Floor
Washington, D.C. 20005
(202) 898-0414

An AIDS information and education agency. NAPWA will provide printed information to people interested in AIDS education. NAPWA also offers medical and counseling referrals and maintain a group of speakers.

The National Coalition of Hispanic Health and Human Services Organizations

1030 15th Street NW
Washington, D.C. 20005
(202) 371-2100

A national organization of health service agencies dedicated to helping the Hispanic community. The Coalition will provide information about many different types of services, including those for people with HIV infection and AIDS.

People With AIDS Coalition

31 West 26th Street
New York, NY 10010
(212) 532-0290

The nation's largest "self-help" group for people with
AIDS/HIV, PWAC offers information and newsletters
about AIDS treatments and current medical events and
provide counseling and referrals to people with AIDS and
their loved ones. They also have an active speakers
bureau and will provide speakers for interested groups.
In addition, PWAC operates a national hotline Monday
through Friday from 10:00 A.M. to 8:00 P.M. The hotline
number is 1-800-828-3280.

San Francisco AIDS Foundation

25 Van Ness Avenue
Suite 660
San Francisco, CA 94102
(415) 864-5855

A large organization that offers a wide range of AIDS-
related services, including information on testing, a food
bank, an emergency housing program, legal counseling,
and medical referrals. They also have a hotline for
Northern California (1-800-367-2437) that is open
9:00 A.M.–9:00 P.M. weekdays and 11:00 A.M.–5:00 P.M. on
weekends.

Sex Information and Education Council of the United States
130 West 42nd Street
Suite 2500
New York, NY 10036
(212) 819-9770

One of the largest sex-education councils in the United States. SIECUS will provide information and referrals on many aspects of sex education, including AIDS.

Wedge Program
1540 Market Street
Suite 435
San Francisco, CA 94102
(415) 554-9098

An AIDS-education program that provides HIV-positive people to speak to groups interested in learning more about HIV and AIDS.

ORGANIZATIONS FOR LESBIAN, GAY, AND BISEXUAL YOUNG PEOPLE

Hetrick-Martin Institute

401 West Street
New York, NY 10014
(212) 633-8920
(212) 633-8926 for the hearing impaired

An agency for bisexual, gay, and lesbian young people ages 12–21. Hetrick-Martin offers free confidential counseling about sexuality issues and HIV support groups and social activities for anyone who wishes to participate.

Los Angeles Gay and Lesbian Community Services Center

1213 North Highland Avenue
Los Angeles, CA 90038
(213) 464-7400
(213) 464-0029 for the hearing impaired
(213) 462-8130 youth talk line
(818) 508-1802 youth talk line for outside Los Angeles

An organization serving the lesbian and gay community, the center offers a wide range of programs specifically for lesbian and gay young people, including rap groups, AIDS education, crisis counseling, substance-abuse counseling, emergency food and shelter programs, help for homeless and runaway teens, a speakers' bureau, a magazine for gay and lesbian youth, and a buddy program. The center also has a unique pen pal program for gay and lesbian teens in areas where there are no gay organizations. If you are interested in participating in this program, you can write to the Pen Pal Program in care of the above address.

Presence and Respect for Youth in Sexual Minorities (PRYSM)

1418 West 29th Street
Cleveland, OH 44113
(216) 781-6736 hotline

PRYSM is a support network for young people dealing with all aspects of sexual identity. It is offered through the Lesbian and Gay Community Services Center of Cleveland.

Sexual Minority Youth Assistance League (SMYAL)

333$^{1}/_{2}$ Pennsylvania Avenue SE
3rd Floor
Washington, D.C. 20003
(202) 546-5940

An organization dedicated to serving young people ages 14–21 dealing with all aspects of sexual identity, including lesbian, gay, bisexual, transexual, and transvestite teens. The league provides training and education programs for people working with sexual identity issues, offers support groups, and provides referrals for medical and counseling issues. They also host social events and will provide speakers on the subject of dealing with youths and sexual identity.

ORGANIZATIONS FOR RUNAWAY AND HOMELESS TEENS

Adolescent Treatment and Education Alliance
2751 Mary Street
La Crescenta, CA 91214
(818) 248-2623

An education program for people ages 12–20. It provides a home for HIV-positive homeless young people ages 12–17 from the Los Angeles County area. The project also trains teens to do outreach programs on the street.

Covenant House
460 West 41st Street
New York, NY 10036
(212) 613-0300

Covenant House is a national organization with offices in many cities. To find the Covenant House nearest you, call 1-800-999-9999. Covenant House provides free AIDS education, referrals, peer counseling, addiction counseling, and street outreach programs. Several offices also offer residential programs for homeless and runaway youth as well as for HIV-positive young people.

National Network of Runaway and Youth Services

1400 I Street
Suite 330
Washington, D.C. 20005
1-800-878-2437

A national organization whose goal is to prevent HIV infection and other related health problems among runaway and homeless youth through the Safe Choices Project. They offer HIV prevention materials, training and assistance to homeless shelters, and programs serving homeless and runaway young people.

National Runaway Switchboard

3080 North Lincoln
Chicago, IL 60657
(312) 880-9860

An organization offering free crisis intervention and counseling for runaway and homeless young people. In addition, they offer a 24-hour, toll-free national hotline. This number is 1-800-621-4000.

Neon Street

3227 North Sheffield
Chicago, IL 60657
(312) 528-7767

A program for homeless people ages 13–21. It offers AIDS education and counseling services as well as sexuality and health education counseling.

Street Work Project

Victim Services Agency
642 10th Avenue
New York, NY 10036
(212) 245-5140

A project offering AIDS education, shelter, food, and referrals to homeless and runaway people under 21. Workers will travel anywhere in New York City between 1:00 P.M. and midnight to meet with teens needing help. Weekend hours are 4:00 P.M.–midnight. The Street Work Project also has a 24-hour runaway line for New York City. It is (212) 619-6884.

Abstinence: Refraining from participating in something. In talking about AIDS, abstinence refers to not participating in sexual activity.

AIDS (Acquired immunodeficiency syndrome): A condition affecting the immune and central nervous systems in which the ability to fight off infections is impaired to the point where various infections and cancers are able to take hold.

Anal sex: Sexual intercourse in which a man's penis enters his partner's anus or rectum.

Anonymous: Without any identification. The term is used in regard to AIDS testing in which the people performing the test do not know the name or identity of the person whose blood they are testing.

Antibodies: Proteins that are manufactured by the immune system to fight off invading substances that may cause disease.

Antibody test: A procedure that tests to see if the immune system has produced any antibodies to specific viruses. An HIV antibody test checks to see if a person's body has produced any antibodies to HIV.

Antigen test: A test that looks for the presence of a virus in someone's body rather than just testing for antibodies to that virus. An antigen test for AIDS looks for HIV.

Antiviral: A drug that works against the actions of a virus. In this case, an antiviral would be used to fight the work of the AIDS virus.

Anus: The opening of the body through which feces, or bowel movements, pass. The anus is the part of the body that is penetrated during anal sex.

Asymptomatic: Being infected with the AIDS virus but not having any symptoms of infection.

AZT: The common name for the drug zidovudine, which is used to treat people with HIV infection.

Bisexual: A person who is sexually attracted to both men and women. A bisexual can be a man or a woman.

Bodily fluids: Any of the fluids produced by or found in the human body, including sweat, urine, blood, tears, breast milk, vaginal fluids, semen, pre-cum, and saliva. Of all the bodily fluids, HIV is found in significant quantities only in blood, semen, vaginal fluids, and breast milk.

Breast milk: The milk produced in a woman's body during pregnancy and secreted through her nipples.

Cardiopulmonary resuscitation: Commonly called CPR. It involves breathing air into the mouth and lungs of a person whose heart has stopped and compressing the chest to massage the heart and circulate blood and oxygen.

Casual contact: Contact with other people that is experienced as a part of everyday, normal activities. In talking about AIDS and how it is spread, casual contact refers to such activities as touching, hugging, kissing, shaking hands with, going to school with, or talking to another person.

Central nervous system: The system of the body that controls sensory and motor functions, including vision and muscle control. The central nervous system is made up of the brain and the spinal cord.

Cervix: The narrow opening to the uterus.

Condom: Commonly called a rubber, a condom is a sheath of latex rubber that fits over a man's penis to prevent his semen from entering his partner's body after ejaculation. A condom also prevents a man's penis from coming into contact with his partner's bodily fluids.

Confidential: Kept secret. In regard to HIV testing, it means that the results of an HIV test are known only to the person who is being tested and the person or facility performing the test.

Contagious: Capable of being spread from one person to another through casual contact.

Contraceptive sponge: A small sponge treated with spermicide that is inserted into a woman's vagina before intercourse to prevent pregnancy.

Cum: The common name for semen, the substance ejaculated by a man during sexual intercourse. The word is also used to describe the act of ejaculation during sexual activity.

ddl: The name for the drug didanosine. It is used to treat people in advanced stages of HIV infection who do not respond to AZT or whose immune systems are severely suppressed.

Dental dam: A sheet of latex rubber that is placed over a woman's vagina during oral sex to prevent her partner's mouth from coming into contact with her vaginal secretions. A dental dam may also be placed over a person's anus during rimming.

Diaphragm: A rubber cup, used along with a spermicide, that is placed in a woman's vagina to block the entrance to her cervix and prevent pregnancy.

Douche: Liquid that is put into a woman's vagina and then expelled in order to flush out any loose material that may be inside. A douche may also be used to rinse out a person's rectum, in which case it is called an enema.

ELISA: The test most commonly used to determine if a person is infected with the AIDS virus. The ELISA test looks for the presence of antibodies to HIV.

Epidemic: An outbreak of a disease that spreads very quickly and is difficult to control. We say that there is an AIDS epidemic because the disease is spreading very quickly to many segments of the population.

False-negative: An incorrect result of an AIDS test in which it is determined that the person being tested has not been infected with the AIDS virus when in fact he or she has.

False-positive: An incorrect result of an AIDS test in which it is determined that the person being tested has been infected with the AIDS virus when in fact he or she has not.

Feces: Bodily wastes that are excreted through the anus.

Fetus: An unborn, developing baby.

Foreskin: The skin that covers the end and tip of a man's penis if he has not been circumcised.

Full-blown AIDS: The term used to describe the condition of a person who has tested positive for HIV and who has developed one or more of a set of indicator diseases recognized by the Centers for Disease Control as being symptoms of HIV infection with immunosuppression.

Gay: A word used to describe someone who is attracted to members of the same sex.

Genetic material: Material found in the cells of living things that is used in reproduction. In regard to AIDS, this is the material in a cell that determines what kind of cell will be created through transcription.

Helper lymphocytes: Another name for T4-lymphocytes. They are called helper lymphocytes because they help organize the other parts of the immune system to fight off invading substances.

Hemophiliac: A male who is suffering from a blood disorder in which a clotting agent is not present in the blood. Hemophiliacs require frequent transfusions of clotting factors. Hemophilia does not affect women.

Heterosexual: A person who is sexually attracted exclusively to people of the opposite sex.

Heterosexual sex: Sexual contact that takes place between people of opposite sexes.

High-risk behavior: The term used to describe any behavior that puts a person in danger of becoming infected with the AIDS virus. This includes anal, oral, and vaginal sex without the use of a condom, and sharing needles to inject intravenous drugs.

HIV (Human immunodeficiency virus): The name of the virus that causes AIDS.

HIV disease: Another name for infection with the AIDS virus.

HIV-positive: The term used to describe someone whose blood has been found to be infected with HIV, the virus that causes AIDS.

Homosexual: A person who is sexually attracted to members of the same sex. A homosexual woman is called a lesbian. Both homosexual men and women are also called gay.

Homosexual sex: Sexual contact that occurs between members of the same sex.

Immune system: The system of the body that fights off infections.

Immunosuppression: A condition in which a person's immune system has been weakened to a point where it no longer functions effectively.

Inconclusive: Not determined definitely one way or another. In this case, the term refers to test results that cannot positively or negatively determine the presence of the AIDS virus.

Incubation period: The length of time between when a person becomes infected with HIV and when the first signs of HIV infection begin to appear.

Indicator diseases: A set of infections and diseases established by the Centers for Disease Control as being indicative of HIV infection. These diseases are used to diagnose a person as having full-blown AIDS.

Intravenous drugs: Drugs that are injected directly into a person's bloodstream through a needle. Also called IV drugs, these include cocaine, crack, and heroin.

Invasive procedure: Any medical procedure, such as an operation or a dental cleaning, that results in exposure to a person's blood.

Kaposi's sarcoma: Also called KS. A type of skin cancer commonly found in people with AIDS. It appears as purplish blotches on the skin.

Killer lymphocytes: Special cells found in the bloodstream that attack and destroy invading substances.

Lesbian: A woman who is sexually attracted to other women.

Lubricant: Any substance that is used to moisten a man's penis, a woman's vagina, or a man's or woman's anus during sexual activity.

Lymph nodes: Glands that are connected to the lymphatic system, a system that carries fluids through the body. When a person is infected with HIV, these areas will sometimes swell. Main lymph nodes are found in the armpits, neck, and groin.

Macrophage: A type of white blood cell important in fighting off infections.

Mandatory testing: Testing that is required. In this case, it refers to the belief that everyone should be tested for the AIDS virus.

Masturbation: Stimulation of a man's penis or a woman's vagina and/or clitoris that doesn't involve penetration.

Menstruation: The time during a woman's reproductive cycle when the uterus discharges an unfertilized egg along with blood, secretions, and tissue. When a woman is menstruating, we say she is having her period.

Monogamous: Having a long-term sexual relationship with only one partner.

Nonoxynol-9: A chemical that is found in some lubricants and condoms. It kills sperm and may help prevent the transmission of the AIDS virus.

Opportunistic infections: Any number of infections that take the opportunity to attack the body of a person whose immune system has been weakened by HIV infection.

Oral sex: Sexual activity in which a person's mouth or tongue comes into contact with a man's penis, a woman's vagina, or a man's or woman's anus.

Pelvic inflammatory disease (PID): A condition in which a woman's groin area becomes swollen and painful as a result of being infected by one of several substances. PID may be an indication of HIV infection.

Penis: The male sexual organ through which urine and semen pass.

***Pneumocystis carinii* pneumonia**: Also called PCP. An opportunistic infection that settles in the lungs.

Pre-cum: The clear fluid that is produced by a man's penis before ejaculation.

Rectum: The end of the intestines. This is the part of the body through which feces, or bowel movements, pass. It is also the part of the body that comes into contact with a man's penis during anal sex.

Rimming: Another word for oral sex in which a person's mouth or tongue comes into contact with a person's anus.

Safer sex: The term used to describe sexual activity that is considered to be low-risk. Safer sex includes touching, sexual intercourse with condoms, massage, and masturbation.

Saliva: Another word for spit, the watery substance formed in the mouth by the salivary glands.

Semen: The milky fluid that is ejaculated from a man's penis. It is commonly refered to as cum.

Seropositive: A term used to describe someone whose blood has tested positively for the presence of HIV.

Sexually transmitted disease: Any disease that is spread through vaginal, anal, or oral sex. Also called STD or VD (venereal disease).

Spermicide: A chemical that kills sperm. Some condoms are coated with spermicides to help prevent transmission of the AIDS virus.

Steroids: Illegal drugs that are injected into the body in order to increase muscle mass. Steroids are most often used by bodybuilders and athletes who want to become stronger more quickly.

Syringe: The hollow plastic tube that is attached to a needle used to inject substances into the body. A syringe and needle used to inject drugs is often called a set or works.

T-cell count: A reading of the number of T4-lymphocytes a person has per millimeter of blood. T-cell count is often used to determine how far along HIV infection is. T-cell count is also used to classify a person as having full-blown AIDS.

T4-lymphocyte: More commonly called a T-cell, a T4-lymphocyte is a type of white blood cell that is important to the immune system in fighting off infections. Also called helper lymphocytes, T4-cells are the type of blood cells most commonly referred to when discussing AIDS.

Thrush: A type of yeast infection that affects the mouth and throat, producing a whitish coating or spots. Thrush may be an early symptom of HIV infection.

Transcription: The process by which a cell reproduces genetic material.

Transfusion: The process by which blood or blood products from one person or group of people are injected into the body of another person.

Transmissible: Capable of passing from one person to another through means other than casual contact.

Tuberculosis: A highly communicable disease that affects the lungs.

Unprotected sex: Vaginal, oral, or anal sex in which a man's penis is not covered with a condom, oral sex in which a woman's vagina is not covered by a dental dam, or rimming in which the recipient's anus is not covered by a dental dam.

Urethra: In a man, the opening in the tip of the penis through which urine and semen pass. The opening through which a woman's urine passes is also called the urethra.

Urine: Liquid body waste that is passed through the urethra.

Vaccine: A substance that is injected into the body to prevent a person from becoming infected with a certain disease.

Vagina: The part of a female's reproductive system that connects the uterus to the outside of the body. During vaginal intercourse, this is the part of the body that comes into contact with a man's penis.

Vaginal secretions: Bodily fluids that are produced in a woman's vagina.

Vaginal sex: Sexual intercourse in which a man's penis penetrates a woman's vagina.

Venereal disease: Another name for a sexually transmitted disease. It is any disease that can be spread through sexual contact.

Viral culture: A test in which laboratory workers actually try to grow HIV from a person's blood or bodily fluids.

Western blot: A test that is used to double check the results of an ELISA test. It tests for the presence of HIV antibodies in blood, bodily fluids, or tissue samples.

Window period: The length of time between when a person has been infected with HIV and when the body has produced enough antibodies to the virus for them to be detected by a blood test. Generally, the window period is between several weeks and six months from the date of infection.

Yeast infection: A type of vaginal infection that is common in women. It creates a whitish discharge. Yeast infections can also occur in the mouth. This is called thrush.

INDEX

precautions against infection with 25, 59, 62-63, 92-98, 104-106
similarity to other viruses of 23
skin as barrier against 25, 59
statistics on infection with 28-31, 66, 67
symptoms of infection with 28-31, 66, 67
T-cells and 22
talking to partners about 67, 68, 142
testing for 30, 127-138 *see also* testing
transcription process and 18
transmission of 23-24, 25, 26, 55, 58, 59, 60, 61, 65-66, 69
transmission through anal sex of 89
transmission through IV drug use of 108-109
transmission through oral sex of 90-91
transmission through vaginal sex of 88-89
vaccine for 41
women and 31
young people and 27-28
HIV disease 17 *see also* AIDS
homeless 27, 37, 38
homosexual sex 88
homosexuals 37, 56-57

I

immune system:
   definition of 15, 21-22
   effects of HIV on 17-19
indicator diseases 32, 33
insects 65
insurance benefits 33, 138
intravenous (IV) drug use 24, 55, 56, 103, 108-109

K

Kaposi's sarcoma 20-21, 140
kissing 55, 107

L

lesbians 56-57
lubricants 95, 97
lymph nodes 29

M

macrophages 18
mandatory testing 137-138
masturbation 92
menstruation 90
mosquito bites 65
mouth-to-mouth resuscitation 64

N

needle cleaning 108-109
nonoxynol-9 97

O

opportunistic infections:
  definition of 19
  examples of 20-21
  use in defining AIDS 32
oral sex 56, 68, 87, 90-91, 92, 93,
  98, 106
organ transplants 63

P

peer pressure 102-104
pelvic inflamatory disease (PID)
  31
penis 24, 87, 88, 90, 91, 93, 94-96
Pneumocystis carinii pneumonia
  (PCP) 20, 140
pre-cum 24, 90, 93, 106

R

rectum 29, 59, 87, 89, 91, 106
rimming 87, 91, 98
rubbers *see* condoms

S

safer sex:
  definition of 92
  kissing 92
  massage 92
  masturbation 92
  talking to partner about 101-
    103
  touching 92
saliva 25, 64, 107
semen 24, 90, 92, 93, 105, 106

sexual activity 24, 55, 61-62 *see*
  also safer sex
anal sex 56, 68, 87, 89, 92, 93,
  95, 106
oral sex 56, 68, 87, 90-91, 93,
  93, 98, 106
safer sex 91, 101-103
vaginal sex 56, 68, 87, 88-89,
  92, 93, 95, 106
sexually transmitted diseases
  (STDs) 87, 91, 93
spermicides 104
  condoms and 104-105
sports 69
steroids 24, 56, 108
sweat 25
syphilis 87, 91

T

T-cell count 18-19, 29-30
T-cells 17-19, 22, 140
T4-lymphocyte *see* T-cells
tattooing 65-66
tears 25
teenagers:
  anal sex and 89
  bisexual and gay 37-38, 57
  fight against AIDS and 147-149
  homeless 37-38
  number infected with HIV 27-
    28
  number with AIDS 36-37, 89
testing: 127-138
  anonymous vs. confidential
    130
  antibody test 131

antigen test 131
attitudes toward 135
dealing with results of 127-128,
139
ELISA test 131, 133
false-negative test result 136
false-positive test result 136
finding a test site 129-130
high-risk activity and 136-137
importance of 30
inconclusive test result 133,
135
laws and 130
mandatory testing 137-138
negative test result 135
positive test result 134
procedure for 132-133, 134
reporting of results of 38
talking with partners about 67,
139
types of tests 131
Western blot test 131, 133
window period and 129
thrush 30
toilet seats 55
transcription 18
transfusions 55, 63, 64
treatment 141-142
tuberculosis 21

U
urethra 88, 89, 91
urine 25

V
vaccines 41
vagina 24, 29, 59, 87, 88, 93, 106
vaginal fluids/secretions 24, 90,
92, 98
vaginal sex 56, 68, 87, 88, 89, 92,
93, 95, 106
venereal disease 87
viral culture test 131, 133 *see also*
testing
viruses 16-17, 21, 22, 23
volunteering 147-149

W
Western blot test 131, 133 *see also*
testing
window period 129, 136
women:
    AIDS and 21, 37, 89
    CDC AIDS definition and 33
    condoms and 99
    HIV infection and 89
    symptoms of HIV infection in
    31
World Health Organization 26

Y
yeast infections 31

Z
zidovudine *see* AZT